GOD'

FOR THE

CHURCH

LOVED,

REDEEMED,

TRANSFORMED,

CALLED

DEREK PRINCE

WHITAKER
HOUSE

God's Vision for the Church:
Loved, Redeemed, Transformed, Called
(abridged from *Rediscovering God's Church*)

Derek Prince Ministries–International
P.O. Box 19501
Charlotte, North Carolina 28219-9501
www.derekprince.org

ISBN: 978-1-64123-908-0
eBook ISBN: 978-1-64123-909-7
Printed in the United States of America
© 2006, 2022 by Derek Prince Ministries–International

Whitaker House
1030 Hunt Valley Circle
New Kensington, PA 15068
www.whitakerhouse.com

The Library of Congress has cataloged the original edition as follows:
Prince, Derek.
Rediscovering God's church / by Derek Prince.
p. cm.
Summary: "Describes God's original blueprint for the church and how today's church can fulfill this calling"—Provided by publisher.
ISBN-13: 978-0-88368-812-0 (trade hardcover : alk. paper)
ISBN-10: 0-88368-812-3 (trade hardcover : alk. paper)
1. Church. I. Title.
BV601.P75 2006
262—dc22   2005035894

1 2 3 4 5 6 7 8 9 10 11 ᵾᵾ 29 28 27 26 25 24 23 22

CONTENTS

INTRODUCTION

"Christ also loved the church and gave Himself for her."
—Ephesians 5:25

Jesus Christ deeply loves the church. His ongoing intercession for us at the Father's right hand (see Hebrews 7:25), just as His earthly ministry was, is for the purpose of:

+ Revealing how we are beloved by our heavenly Father
+ Redeeming us from sin and estrangement from God
+ Transforming us into His image
+ Calling us to unity and equipping us for His divine purposes

As much as any teacher of modern times, Derek Prince understood the greatness to which the body of Christ is called and destined. Following the example of Christ, to whom he was devoted, Derek loved and served the church in Jesus's name, teaching people the fullness of God's vision for His people.

Derek's understanding of God's purposes for the church came from his in-depth study of the Scriptures, his involvement in local bodies of believers, and his travels to teach at churches and other gatherings of Christians in many nations throughout the world. He also lived and worked in various areas of the globe, including England, the United States, Israel, and East Africa, seeing firsthand how the truths of the Bible concerning the church are universally applicable in many distinct cultures. He saw the church from a global persective, which was a rare gift. Thus, what you will find in this book is an extraordinary depth of revelation about the nature, role, and destiny of the church—both local and universal. And, as you read, you'll also gain fresh insights into *your* specific place and part in God's plan for the church and His purposes in history.

God's vision for the church is that His people not merely be a group of individuals but that we become a single whole, functioning as a unified body as we minister God's grace in the world. The daily life of the local church is to be an example of a people living and working in harmony to fulfill God's grand vision. Derek encourages us, "What we become *together* is the final goal." He further wrote,

> Jesus's ultimate vision is to blend individuals from every race and background into visible unity. The world sees things in time and space; it does not see mystical realities of a spirit realm. If we are going to reach the world with God's redemptive message, we must be visible—something the world can see and appreciate. Thus, we cannot hide or downplay our Christianity, because God's purpose is to bring His people to become *visibly* united. And this unity will be irrefutable testimony to the entire world that God indeed sent Jesus. As we come to be a true reflection of God's redemptive people, others will also be drawn to Him in personal relationship

and will join us in becoming His own special treasure for all of eternity.

Learning about God's vision for the church is heartening and exciting—and it is also very challenging. But Derek reassures us:

> Scripture compares God's Word to a mirror that reveals our inward spiritual condition so that we may see ourselves as God sees us: all the way to the end result—not only as we should be, but as we will be....
>
> In this book, we will look into the mirror of God's Word so we can learn what we are like in God's sight as His collective people.

The overall picture of the church that unfolds is that of a people who are *loved, redeemed, chosen,* and *called.* May God bless you as enter into the fullness of being a loved and valued member of Christ's body on earth.

—*The International Publishing Team of Derek Prince Ministries*

PART 1:

GOD'S REDEMPTIVE PEOPLE

1

GOD'S PORTION IS
HIS PEOPLE

One of the grandest themes of Scripture is the church—the object of God's affection, the future bride for His beloved Son.

Christ's redemptive mission on earth is a love story, played out on the stages of time and eternity, and filled with drama, pathos, love, struggle, and triumph. God's intention is to provide for His Son a perfect companion for all eternity.

The church is also God's redemptive agent in the world. But His challenge is the very people who comprise the church. He must get us, in our unruly condition, to become the perfect bride of His only Son.

The Mirror of God's Word

Scripture compares God's Word to a mirror that reveals our inward spiritual condition so that we may see ourselves as God sees us: all the way to the end result—not only as we should be, but as we will be.

> *The LORD does not see as man sees; for man looks at the outward appearance, but the LORD looks at the heart.* (1 Samuel 16:7)

If we look into this mirror before we have been reconciled to God through Jesus Christ, it shows us our unclean and sinful condition. Once we have been reconciled to God and cleansed from our sin, it shows us what we have become as God's new creation in Christ. We experience in a personal way these truths of Scripture:

> *Therefore, if anyone is in Christ, he is a new creation; old things have passed away; behold, all things have become new.*
> (2 Corinthians 5:17)

> *For we are His workmanship, created in Christ Jesus for good works, which God prepared beforehand that we should walk in them.*
> (Ephesians 2:10)

In this book, we will look into the mirror of God's Word so we can learn what we are like in God's sight as His collective people. We will examine the seven pictures of God's people as revealed by the apostle Paul in the book of Ephesians. From there, we will explore the lifestyle and future of the church.

GOD'S FINAL OBJECTIVE IS NOT JUST REDEEMED PEOPLE; HIS GOAL IS A SPECIAL PEOPLE.

God's Redemptive Purposes

God's purposes in redeeming His people to Himself are found in the book of Exodus:

> And Moses went up to God, and the LORD called to him from the mountain, saying, "Thus you shall say to the house of Jacob and tell the sons of Israel: 'You yourselves have seen what I did to the Egyptians, and how I bore you on eagles' wings, and brought you to Myself. Now then, if you will indeed obey My voice and keep My covenant, then you shall be My own possession among all the peoples, for all the earth is Mine.'" (Exodus 19:3–5 NASB)

There are two primary objects of redemption as revealed in these words of God to Israel.

A Direct, Personal Relationship with God

First, notice what God said about the actual act of redemption: "*You yourselves have seen what I did to the Egyptians, and how I bore you on eagles' wings, and brought you to Myself*" (Exodus 19:4). This Scripture reveals that God brings the redeemed to Himself. His first purpose of redemption is to bring His redeemed people into a direct, personal relationship with Him. It is surprising how few people in the Old Testament period seemed to grasp this concept. They were interested in the Law, the material blessings, and the promised land. They were looking at *things*, which is why most of them missed out on a wonderful, direct, personal relationship with God. Even today, many people do not seem to fully understand that the primary purpose of God is to *bring us to Himself*. Everything else is secondary.

His Own Possession

The second purpose of redemption is for God to make the redeemed into His own possession. The phrase translated as *"My own possession"* in Exodus 19:5 (NASB) is from a Hebrew word for which the exact meaning is unknown. Other translations use the phrases *"a special treasure to Me"* (NKJV), *"my treasured possession"* (NIV), and *"a peculiar treasure unto me"* (KJV). The indication is that God wants to make us something *personal, peculiar, special.* It is rather exciting that we do not know the exact meaning of the original Hebrew term because it leaves open so many possibilities. But we do know that it is something beautiful, far above the level of what we could imagine or think for ourselves. That is why He redeemed us.

A NEW PEOPLE

God *invests in people.* He is much more concerned about people than about things. This truth is illustrated beautifully and simply in Deuteronomy 32:9: *"For the LORD's portion is His people."* God's purpose centers on His redeemed people—His portion in all that has happened and is happening in the world. Yet we must clearly understand that His ultimate goal is not only to redeem individuals; it is also the creation of a special *people,* a single, new, organic *whole*—something vastly different from what existed among peoples before God intervened through redemption.

Contemporary Christianity places most of the emphasis on the individual and his or her relationship with God. While this is very important, the final objective of God is not just redeemed individuals; His goal is a *special people.*

In His prayer to His Father, Jesus revealed to us tremendous insight into the particular stage in God's purposes in which we are living today:

> *I do not pray for these alone, but also for those who will believe in Me through their word; that they all may be one, as You, Father, are in Me, and I in You; that they also may be one in Us, that the world may believe that You sent Me. And the glory which You gave Me I have given them, that they may be one just as We are one: I in them and You in Me; that they may be made perfect [or complete] in one, and*

that the world may know that You have sent Me, and have loved them
as You have loved Me.   (John 17:20–23)

Jesus's ultimate vision is to blend individuals from every race and background into visible unity. The world sees things in time and space; it does not see mystical realities of a spirit realm. If we are going to reach the world with God's redemptive message, we must be visible—something the world can see and appreciate. Thus, we cannot hide or downplay our Christianity, because God's purpose is to bring His people to become *visibly* united. And this unity will be irrefutable testimony to the entire world that God indeed sent Jesus. As we come to be a true reflection of God's redemptive people, others will also be drawn to Him in personal relationship and will join us in becoming His own special treasure for all of eternity.

2

TRANSFORMATION: GOD'S PROGRAM FOR THE CHURCH

In order for God to make us into the kind of people He intends us to become, there must be a process of transformation. When God first redeems us, we are only beginning the journey toward all that we ought to be and that God intends us to be. I marvel at God's faith in even taking on this project of transforming people like me!

The Process of Transformation

As an example of how the process of transformation works, take a look at the call of Jesus to His first disciples:

And Jesus, walking by the Sea of Galilee, saw two brothers, Simon called Peter, and Andrew his brother, casting a net into the sea; for they were fishermen. Then He said to them, "Follow Me, and I will make you fishers of men." They immediately left their nets and followed Him. (Matthew 4:18–20)

This simple scene does not contain a lot of complicated psychology, but just the essence of what has to happen. There are two main components to Jesus saying, *"Follow Me, and I will make you fishers of men."*

Total Commitment

First, Jesus requires *total* commitment. "Leave it all; follow Me. I'm not telling you where we're going; you just have to follow Me in faith. Put your life in My hands and let Me take care of the consequences." That is essential. God cannot really work His purposes until His people are fully committed.

Then, Jesus says, "I'm not telling you where we're going, but I am telling you what I will make of you. I will make you fishers of men." The important thing with every one of God's redeemed people is not what we are right now but what God wants to make of us. If we yield to the Lord, He guarantees the finished product. But first we must commit ourselves to God's purpose, and then He begins to work in us to make us into what He wants us to be.

The same principle is inherent in the teaching of Paul:

I beseech you therefore, brethren, by the mercies of God, that you present your bodies a living sacrifice, holy, acceptable to God, which is your reasonable service. And do not be conformed to this world, but be transformed by the renewing of your mind, that you may prove what is that good and acceptable and perfect will of God. (Romans 12:1–2)

As we saw in Matthew 4:18–20, the first step to God's transforming process within us is *total commitment to God*. Paul expressed this truth in the words, *"Present your bodies a living sacrifice."* He was thinking in terms of the Old Testament sacrifices of animals, such as sheep and bulls, which were killed and then placed as an offering on God's altar. Once they were placed on God's altar, they no longer belonged to the person who offered them; they belonged to God alone. Paul was telling us Christians that we have to offer our own bodies to God in exactly the same way. Once you have placed your body on the altar, it no longer belongs to you; it belongs entirely to God. But there's one major difference: Your body won't be killed first; it'll be placed live on the altar! Now *that's* total commitment.

Transformation from Within

Commitment to God leads us to think in a higher way. When our minds become *renewed*, our values change and our priorities are altered. Things take on a different meaning. That is something God does only for the committed. When we are transformed by the renewing of our minds, we are able to discern and approve God's will. We *can* find out what He really wants. He has a wonderful plan for each of us individually and for His people collectively, but He reveals His plans only to those who are committed.

> But we all, with unveiled face, beholding as in a mirror the glory of the
> Lord, are being transformed into the same image from glory to glory,
> just as by the Spirit of the Lord.   (2 Corinthians 3:18)

Remember, God's Word is a mirror that shows us what we are *inwardly*. This mirror is an essential instrument in the process of transformation. Notice that the above Scripture is written in the plural. It is not just for individuals; it's for us *all*. It shows us what God intends for all His believing people collectively. Without this view of God's people as a single whole, we tend to get lost in our own needs and problems and blessings, and we miss the larger, overall plan and purposes of God. "We fail to see the forest for the trees," as the saying goes.

Transformed from Glory to Glory

As we reflect on the mirror of God's Word, we behold the glory that God is going to work in *us*. As we behold this glory by faith and continue looking in the mirror of God's Word, the Spirit of God transforms us into the likeness of what we see—but only if we look *by faith* into the mirror. If we do not look in the mirror, the Spirit of God cannot work on us. This is not just one single transformation but "*from glory to glory*"! Each time we arrive at a certain level, God shows us there is a higher level and urges us to move upward.

This transformation depends on two things. First, it depends on our looking by faith into the mirror of God's Word. Second, it rests on the work of the Holy Spirit when we look into the mirror. Each one of us must look regularly into the mirror of God's Word to check on our own personal spiritual condition and relationship to God.

So here is the order of transformation: commitment, then transformation from within, which leads to the revelation of God's purpose.

> For our light affliction, which is but for a moment, is working for us a far more exceeding and eternal weight of glory, while we do not look at the things which are seen, but at the things which are not seen. For the things which are seen are temporary, but the things which are not seen are eternal. (2 Corinthians 4:17–18)

Paul said that we go through affliction as part of the process of transformation. But the affliction will benefit us and will work out God's purposes for us—*if* we continue to focus on the unseen things and not on the visible circumstances and situations swirling around us.

LOOKING INTO THE MIRROR OF GOD'S WORD IS AN ESSENTIAL PART OF THE PROCESS OF TRANSFORMATION.

The things that are seen, Paul said, are temporary; the unseen things are eternal. The way we see the unseen eternal realities of God's purposes for us is to look by faith into the mirror of God's Word. When we do that, the Holy Spirit reveals the destiny God has for us—where He is taking us and what He desires to produce in us and from us. As we keep on looking by faith, not taking our eyes off the mirror, the Holy Spirit continues to change us into that which we have apprehended by faith. Each time we newly apprehend truth by faith, we experience a further transformation. This is the process that takes us truly from glory to glory!

PART 2:

THE NATURE OF THE CHURCH: SEVEN PICTURES OF THE CHURCH IN EPHESIANS

3

PICTURE #1:
THE ASSEMBLY

*"[God] put all things under [Jesus's] feet,
and gave [Jesus] to be head over all things to the church."*
—Ephesians 1:22

In the next few chapters, we will be examining seven pictures of God's people from Paul's epistle to the Ephesians, the first being the assembly.

The Greek word translated *"church"* in Ephesians 1:22 is *ecclesia*, from which we get such English words as *ecclesiology*. The noun *ecclesia* is derived from a verb that means "to call out." The concept is a group of people that is formed by being called out from a larger group of people. It is also a group called out for a special purpose, which applies to the church. We are called out of the world through faith in Jesus Christ for a special purpose of God.

In the contemporary secular Greek of New Testament times, the word *ecclesia* had a very specific meaning. It meant a "governmental assembly." It is used in that way three times in the nineteenth chapter of Acts, where we read about an uproar that broke out in the city of Ephesus because of Paul's ministry.

Note the use of the word *assembly* in Acts 19:

Some therefore cried one thing and some another, for the assembly [ecclesia] was confused, and most of them did not know why they had come together.   (verse 32)

The people were holding an unorganized, unauthorized meeting, and the town clerk rebuked them and told them they had no right to hold a meeting there in that way. Then the clerk added,

But if you have any other inquiry to make, it shall be determined in the lawful assembly [ecclesia].   (verse 39)

The word is used again in verse 41:

And when he had said these things, he dismissed the assembly [ecclesia].

Thus, the root meaning of the word we habitually translate as *church* actually means "a legal or governmental assembly."

In this chapter, I am going to stick to the word *assembly* in translating the word for church. This meaning has been obliterated by many modern translations, but *the governmental assembly* is the first picture of God's people in the mirror of God's Word.

Qualifications to Enter the Assembly

In the Greek assembly in Ephesus, many people were excluded: slaves (who comprised nearly half of the population), women, and all visitors and temporary residents. The assembly was reserved only for free citizens residing in Ephesus.

What are the qualifications to be in the assembly of the Lord Jesus Christ? Jesus Himself told us:

> [Jesus] *said to them, "But who do you say that I am?" Simon Peter answered and said, "You are the Christ, the Son of the living God." Jesus answered and said to him, "Blessed are you, Simon Bar-Jonah, for flesh and blood has not revealed this to you, but My Father who is in heaven. And I also say to you that you are Peter, and on this rock I will build My church, and the gates of Hades shall not prevail against it."* (Matthew 16:15–18)

Peter came out boldly and proclaimed to Jesus, *"You are the Christ* [Messiah], *the Son of the living God."* This revelation did not come by Peter's natural reasoning or logic. It came from God the Father through the Holy Spirit. It did not reveal Jesus of Nazareth as the carpenter's son, whom he already knew, but it revealed Jesus in His divine, eternal nature as the Son of God, the Messiah.

I believe that millions today have been given membership in churches when they have not received this basic revelation. Thus, the church cannot function in its full authority because its members don't even qualify to enter the assembly!

The language of Jesus in the above passage is very emphatic: *"You are Peter, and on this rock I will build My church."* All the emphasis is on the word *"My."* My church, My assembly. Jesus was saying, in effect, that there are many assemblies. Each city and state has its assembly. Nations have their assemblies. But Jesus said, "I am now building *My* assembly." There is a relationship between *build* and *My.* If Jesus doesn't build it, He will not own it. He owns only what He builds.

Once, a preacher was speaking on the gifts of the Holy Spirit. At the end of his message, a lady came up to him and said, "Brother, we don't have these gifts in our church." He said, "Well, they have them in the church of

Jesus Christ. Which is your church?" That's an important and far-reaching question. Which is your church? Is it *His* church?

> *THE CHURCH AS AN ASSEMBLY IS A GROUP CALLED OUT FOR A SPECIAL PURPOSE OF GOD.*

There are four elements that constitute the procedure for admission to the assembly of Jesus Christ: confrontation, revelation, acknowledgement, and confession. We can never enter the assembly to rule until we have had a life-shaking, personal encounter with Jesus, as Peter had before his proclamation of who Jesus is. And we cannot know the truth about Jesus unless it is revealed to us.

Since Jesus made Peter the example, let's use what transpired between the two of them to illustrate the procedure.

There is a *direct confrontation*: Peter met Jesus face-to-face. There was nobody between them, no mediator, no middleman.

There is a *revelation granted*: The revelation was granted by God the Father through the Holy Spirit. Without that revelation, Peter could not have known who Jesus truly is.

There is an *acknowledgement of the revelation*: Peter acknowledged the revelation when he responded to Christ's question.

There is a *confession of the revelation*: Peter confessed, out loud, *"You are the Christ, the Son of the living God."*

The Church as Zion

In Scripture, the title that is regularly used for the assembly of God's people when they meet in divine order is *Zion*. Let's examine what the Scripture says about Zion and our relationship to Zion as believers:

But you have come to Mount Zion and to the city of the living God, the heavenly Jerusalem, to an innumerable company of angels, to the general assembly and church of the firstborn who are registered in heaven, to God the Judge of all, to the spirits of just men made perfect, to Jesus the Mediator of the new covenant, and to the blood of sprinkling that speaks better things than that of Abel. (Hebrews 12:22–24)

Notice that this is not a future event. The writer did not say, "You are soon going to come." He said that you have already come! Not physically, of course, but spiritually, we are already part of the total governmental assembly of God. Although part of it is in heaven and part of it is on earth, we are all *one* assembly. Included in that assembly are *"thousands upon thousands of angels in joyful assembly* [or festal array]" (NIV). It's a supremely dignified, glorious assembly.

I recall an incident that occurred at a commanding officer's parade during my years in the military. Everybody had to polish all their pieces of brass and their boots, and stand at attention. There was a military band, and everything was precise and official and dignified. There was an air of *authority*. That is the picture here of Zion, and we are part of it!

Through our faith in Jesus Christ, we are part of the great governmental assembly that governs the entire universe. The Head of that assembly, under God the Father, is Jesus Christ. We, as the church (God's people, the assembly), are the representatives of God's authority in the earth.

Our Earthly Authority

One of the Old Testament verses most quoted in the New Testament presents the tremendous authority of the assembly of the Lord:

The LORD said to my Lord, "Sit at My right hand, till I make Your enemies Your footstool." (Psalm 110:1)

In Mark 12:35–37, Jesus applied the above reference to Himself. *"The LORD"* is God the Father. *"My Lord"* is David's Greater Son, the Lord Jesus Christ. This verse refers to a statement the Father says to the Son after

Jesus's death and resurrection, when He has ascended and taken His place at the Father's right hand. God the Father says to Jesus Christ the Son, "*Sit at My right hand.*" All authority in heaven and in earth has been given to Jesus until God makes all His enemies His footstool.

THE ESSENTIAL FEATURE OF THE ASSEMBLY IS GOVERNMENTAL AUTHORITY.

The New Testament clearly reveals that Jesus is *right now* seated at God's right hand. (See, for example, Romans 8:34; Ephesians 1:20; Colossians 3:1; Hebrews 1:3; 1 Peter 3:22.) Jesus Christ is on His throne right now. And here is how His authority is to be executed on earth:

> *The LORD shall send the rod of Your strength out of Zion. Rule in the midst of Your enemies!* (Psalm 110:2)

I believe that all three persons of the Godhead are represented in the first two verses of Psalm 110. In the first verse, we read that God the Father says to Jesus the Son, "*Sit at My right hand.*" Then, in the second verse, we see that God the Holy Spirit stretches forth the scepter of Christ's authority from Zion, the assembly of His people, and says, "*Rule in the midst of Your enemies!*" Sometimes, we are so conscious of the enemies that we forget that Christ is *already* ruling. His enemies have not all been subdued under His feet yet, but He is ruling supreme in the midst of His enemies—right now, through us! The Holy Spirit extends the scepter of Christ's authority over the nations, kings, and rulers of this earth. And He does this out of the assembly of God's people who are met in divine order through prayer, the ministry of the Word, and the gifts of the Spirit.

Jesus rules *"out of Zion,"* which is the picture of God's people meeting in divine assembly, divine order, and divine authority. God the Father says to God the Son, "All authority is Yours. From now on, You're ruling." But His rule is exercised by the Spirit "out of Zion," the assembly of God's people. We are that rod stretched forth in the Lord's hand representing His authority in whatever sphere we operate! Oh, if we would only grasp the solemnity and power of that truth.

Most Christians accept the fact that Jesus is going to rule someday. But it is vital to know that He is ruling *right now*. When you fully grasp that fact, it will drastically change the way you live. Through our prayers, intercession, and fasting, through our proclamation of the gospel and our committed lifestyle, we are being utilized by Christ to "rule in the midst of His enemies."

Christians are like the rod of Moses in the story of Israel's deliverance from Egypt. The rod is a symbol of authority. The final deliverance of God's people could not take place before Moses learned to use his rod. Likewise, the completion of the destiny of God's people will not take place until we learn to "use the rod," or to function in a unified, governmental way as the assembly, the governing body of God—not in the age to come, but now.

After giving a strong exhortation about right relationships in the church, Jesus said,

> *Assuredly, I say to you, whatever you bind on earth will be bound in heaven, and whatever you loose on earth will be loosed in heaven. Again I say to you that if two of you agree on earth concerning anything that they ask, it will be done for them by My Father in heaven. For where two or three are gathered together in My name, I am there in the midst of them.* (Matthew 18:18–20)

In this passage, notice that the initiative is not with heaven but with earth. When we agree on earth, heaven does the work. When we bind or loose on earth, it is bound or loosed in heaven. Our agreeing and binding and loosing are made effective as we **gather together in a *unified* assembly.**

Heaven takes notice of our requests and our petitions and makes them effective. We have incredible authority as the ruling assembly of God!

I knew a young pastor in Denmark who was facing the problem of divorced people wanting to remarry. He had refused to marry one couple but consented to marry another, and he was being criticized for it. He was not sure if he was doing the right thing, so he took time off to seek the Lord on the issue. He prayed, "Lord, why didn't You make clear in the New Testament Your standards for marriage and divorce and remarriage?" The Lord answered him, "If I'd given you a set of rules, you would have just used them legalistically to bring people into bondage, and you would have shown no mercy." So the pastor said, "Lord, if You'll just show me what *You* would do, then I'll do that." The Lord responded, "On the contrary, if you'll decide what *you* will do, I'll do that."

That is precisely what Matthew 18 says: Whatever you bind, I'll bind; whatever you loose, I'll loose; if you agree, I'll do it. God has placed the responsibility on us, the assembly. He says, "You make the decrees, and I'll enforce them. You make the decisions, and I'll see that they're carried out."

Your Giftings

Another very important point about the assembly is that it functions only when we recognize each other's gifting.

> *As each one has received a gift, minister it to one another, as good stewards of the manifold grace of God. If anyone speaks, let him speak as the oracles of God. If anyone ministers [or serves], let him do it as with the ability which God supplies, that in all things God may be glorified through Jesus Christ, to whom belong the glory and the dominion forever and ever. Amen.* (1 Peter 4:10–11)

What has God made you? What is your office, your function? Every person has a gift (Greek, *charisma*). We must be sensitive to—and minister to one another through—our *charisma*, whether our gifts are speaking, serving, teaching, or anything else.

In my opinion, leadership is also a charisma. The gift of leadership is very recognizable. The ability to lead is something that God places upon a person by the Holy Spirit for a purpose. Or your charisma might be a particular service. One of the great missing ingredients in Christian life today is serving others.

We need to be much more sensitive to the charisma of our brothers and sisters in the church. We should recognize their offices, functions, and places in the assembly.

> *And we urge you, brethren, to recognize those who labor among you, and are over you in the Lord and admonish* [or correct] *you, and to esteem them very highly in love for their work's sake.*
>
> (1 Thessalonians 5:12–13)

Spiritual authority can operate only by voluntary recognition. It cannot be imposed; it must be submitted to. Without submission, there is no spiritual authority.

The work of those in spiritual authority is to admonish the believers, straighten them out, correct them, tell them when they are doing wrong. It takes a true friend to do that. There is nothing more sobering than having somebody tell you, "I accept your authority." People who look to me for leadership place a tremendous and very solemn responsibility upon me.

I want to challenge you to a more serious commitment to the church. No one would ever act casually and without discipline in a legal setting, such as a courtroom, and yet many Christians do so in the church assembly, which is a higher court than any earthly assembly. Attend church consistently and punctually, dress appropriately, serve in some capacity, and appreciate the fact that you are a part of an important institution. Give the assembly your very best in attitude and service.

The Essential Feature of the Assembly and God's Requirement

With each of the seven pictures of the church, I will give you a twofold application: I will point out both the essential feature of each picture and what is required of us as God's people.

The essential feature of the assembly is governmental authority. God has deposited much governmental authority in His assembly. What is required of us in order to exercise God's authority is *respect for God's order.* We cannot govern others if we cannot govern ourselves.

Have you ever attended a conference or meeting where the leader was trying to call the meeting to order, but everybody kept on talking, paying no attention to him? Members are independently carrying on their own conversations and are busy with their own agendas—not to mention showing disrespect for the authority of the leader—so that nothing can be accomplished. Who would want to put a group like that in charge of anything? Yet I wonder if this is the picture of the church that many of our critics have.

We will not be fit to govern the world until we have learned to govern ourselves. Yet God *has* destined us to govern ourselves and also to be the instrument of His government in the earth. What a challenging image we see in the mirror, and what a position we must rise to!

Once you establish a heart of dedication to the assembly, you must pursue the next aspect of relationship to the church: membership in the body of Christ.

4

PICTURE #2:
THE BODY OF CHRIST

"And [God]...gave [Jesus] to be head over all things to the church,
which is His body, the fullness of Him who fills all in all."
—Ephesians 1:22–23

Building on the image of the church as God's governmental assembly of believers, the second picture is that of His body, the body of Christ.

We relate to the world we live in through our bodies. It is in the body that we get things done in a world of time and space. Similarly, Christ relates to the world through us, His body. We are the instruments by which He works out His redemptive purposes in the world.

> *Therefore, when Christ came into the world, he said: "Sacrifice and*
> *offering you did not desire, but a body you prepared for me; with burnt*
> *offerings and sin offerings you were not pleased. Then I said, 'Here I*
> *am—it is written about me in the scroll—I have come to do your will,*
> *O God.'"*   (Hebrews 10:5–7 NIV)

This passage pictures Jesus coming to the earth not to introduce the
Law (which had already been introduced by Moses) but to save us by being
the sacrifice for our sins. In order to do that, He had to have a body with
which to provide a sacrifice.

When put together, these two phrases, *"a body you prepared for me"*
and *"to do your will, O God,"* tell us that the function of the body is to be
the instrument used to accomplish God's will. This displays the twofold
aspect of Christ's body: first, the physical body of Jesus became the sacrifice
for our sins on the cross; and second, the body of God's collective people
continues and completes His ministry on the earth.

The New Testament presents several pictures of believers as the body
of Christ. Paul wrote in Romans,

> *Just as each of us has one body with many members, and these members*
> *do not all have the same function, so in Christ we who are many form*
> *one body, and each member belongs to all the others.*
>   (Romans 12:4–5 NIV)

This body is not a group of separated, isolated individuals. We belong
to one another.

In 1 Corinthians, Paul amplified this picture of the body of Christ:

> *The body is a unit, though it is made up of many parts; and though*
> *all its parts are many, they form one body. So it is with Christ. For we*
> *were all baptized by one Spirit into one body—whether Jews or Greeks,*
> *slave or free—and we were all given the one Spirit to drink.*
>   (1 Corinthians 12:12–13 NIV)

The word emphasized in the above passage is *one*: "*They form* **one** *body.... We were all baptized by* **one** *Spirit into* **one** *body.... We were all given the* **one** *Spirit to drink.*" The emphasis throughout is the *unity of the body.* Paul continued,

> *Now the body is not made up of one part but of many. If the foot should say, "Because I am not a hand, I do not belong to the body," it would not for that reason cease to be part of the body. And if the ear should say, "Because I am not an eye, I do not belong to the body," it would not for that reason cease to be part of the body. If the whole body were an eye, where would the sense of hearing be? If the whole body were an ear, where would the sense of smell be? But in fact God has arranged the parts in the body, every one of them, just as he wanted them to be. If they were all one part, where would the body be? As it is, there are many parts, but one body. The eye cannot say to the hand, "I don't need you!" And the head cannot say to the feet, "I don't need you!"*
>
> (1 Corinthians 12:14–21 NIV)

In our relationships with one another, the word I believe applies best is *interdependent.* The essence of Paul's teaching is that every member needs all the other members. None of us is independent; we cannot do without one another. Therefore, we cannot say to other believers, "I can get along without you. It doesn't matter what happens to you; I'm all right." That attitude is neither permissible nor correct because God has sovereign control over the body. The eye, though it is a wonderful, refined, delicate instrument with more than three million moving, working parts, cannot say to that rather prosaic member, the hand, "I don't need you." Even more remarkably, the head cannot say to the feet, "I don't need you." The head is right at the top, the feet are down at the bottom, and the whole length of the body separates them. Yet they clearly need each other in order for the body to operate with optimum efficiency.

What is significant is that, in a certain sense, the head typifies Jesus. Therefore, Jesus would not say to the lowest part of His body, "I don't need you." Rather, He needs us because we are His body, the instruments He uses to get things done in this world.

The weakest members are actually the most important. No outward part of the body is more frail and sensitive than the eye, yet perhaps none is more important. Notice how carefully nature has protected the eye. It gets all that protection and honor not because it is strong but because it is weak. Here is the way that the body has been knit together. The strong has to protect the weak. We cannot ignore or despise any member of the body of Christ. This is a vital lesson.

When I was a missionary in East Africa, people would come to my door every day from six in the morning until ten at night. I got tired of telling them that I could not do the many things they requested, even in my own field of education. Sometimes, when I had reached the point of real irritation, it was as if the Lord was saying to me, "Now, take care, because you are talking to one of My children." I would have to stop and remember that I had no right to be irritated, impatient, or contemptuous of any child of God. This is true of the members of the body. We need one another, we depend on one another, and we are compelled to honor one another. When one member suffers, the others suffer with it. When one member is honored, the others are honored with it. So it is with the universal body of Jesus Christ, the church.

The Complete Body

> From [Christ] *the whole body, joined and held together by every sup-*
> *porting ligament, grows and builds itself up in love, as each part does*
> *its work.*   (Ephesians 4:16 NIV)

This verse pictures the finished product. Though there are many joints and ligaments that hold us firmly intact, all of us together who are united in Christ are one body. As we are held together in this single, organic unity, the body builds itself up. But, to build itself up, the body depends on each part to do its work. One unhealthy part affects the health of the rest of the body.

What is required to keep all the parts healthy in our relationship with Christ? The words *obedience, submission,* and *willingness* come to mind, but the word I choose is *availability*. The members must be available to the Head. No matter how strong and useful my arm is, it's no good to the head unless it is available to do what the head wants. The same goes for every other part of my body. There is a saying that the only kind of ability God looks for in a person is *avail*ability.

> *Holding fast to the Head, from whom all the body, nourished and knit*
> *together by joints and ligaments, grows with the increase that is from*
> *God.*   (Colossians 2:19)

The "*joints*" are the interrelationships between the various members of the body, through which God's supply comes. My relationship with you is my "joint" with you. It is crucial to understand that our needs are supplied through the joints, or relationships, within the body.

"*Ligaments*" are needed to keep the joints together. A *ligament* is committed, covenant love—love that is committed to another person, like a man to his wife ("for better, for worse," "in sickness and in health"). If I disagree with my wife's doctrine, do I go find another wife? Of course not. When a man is committed to a woman by marriage, it is in spite of disagreements, tensions, and problems. Any marriage that is committed only while there is no tension or problems will not last. What is needed is something that will hold the people together in spite of the tensions and the problems. What is the answer? *Covenant commitment*: a deep, permanent, individual commitment.

We do not get our needs met through the Head alone but through the network of joints and ligaments throughout the body, which are all linked in various ways to the Head. The Head may have made full provision for every need of every member, but the members will not have their needs supplied unless they are rightly related to the other members through the Head.

Since spiritual "nourishment" is supplied through both joints and ligaments, we cannot say, "I'll get everything I need from the Lord alone." The Lord hasn't arranged the body in that way. He has arranged the body so that we must have many of our needs met by our fellow members.

It is remarkable that, on the cross, Jesus did not suffer one bone being broken. Yet the Bible says that all His bones were out of joint. (See Psalm 22:14.) This is how it is with the church; but by God's grace, the bones hold together even if the relationships within the body need a lot of work!

Discovering Your Place

It is important to discover your real place in the body. As I wrote earlier, I have found that the most practical pattern for discovering one's place is found in Romans 12:

> *I beseech you therefore, brethren, by the mercies of God, that you present your bodies a living sacrifice, holy, acceptable to God, which is your reasonable service. And do not be conformed to this world, but be transformed by the renewing of your mind, that you may prove what is that good and acceptable and perfect will of God.* (Romans 12:1–2)

Let's examine the four steps laid out in these verses.

1. Present Your Body

Again, this passage speaks of *"a living sacrifice,"* in contrast with the sacrifices of the Old Testament where the sacrificial offering was killed and placed on the altar. The call to be a living sacrifice raises a deep and far-reaching question that we must each resolve: who owns your body? Settle the question of your body's ownership. If you own it, then the Lord does not. If the Lord owns it, then you do not. Have you ever really presented your body to the Lord and renounced your claim of ownership over it? If not, the time has come.

2. Renew Your Mind

Once you present your body, the second phase of discovering your place in Christ's body occurs: *you begin to think differently.* Natural, unregenerate man is self-centered. He always asks, "What will this do for me? What will I get out of this? Will I enjoy this? Will this promote me?" But we cannot find God's will until our entire way of thinking has been changed.

Scripture says that a carnal mind is at enmity with God, and He does not reveal His will to His enemies but only to His friends. (See Romans 8:7.)

3. Discover the Will of God

As your mind is renewed, you start to discover the will of God, and you begin to enter into His will for your life. In fact, the further you go in the will of God, the better it gets! As the verse states, it is first *"good"*—something that you can intellectually accept as positive. The next stage is *"acceptable,"* in which you really settle in and embrace the will of God. Finally, it becomes *"perfect"* in the sense that you cannot imagine anything more fitting or pleasing!

It is only the renewed mind that finds the will of God. Many Christians stumble and grope through life, never really finding God's will, because they have never been renewed in their minds.

4. Put Away Independence

I believe that a primary emphasis of the Holy Spirit to God's people today is that we must give up our aggressive individualism and negative, incorrect attitudes toward our fellow believers. Again, not one of us can say to any of the others, "I don't need you." God's purposes will not be complete until the body is complete—until all the members are united, with every part doing its job, and the body is growing together in health and glorifying Him.

ALL OF US TOGETHER WHO ARE UNITED IN CHRIST ARE ONE BODY.

I am an independent person, but I am not a "lone ranger" Christian. I have always been closely associated with a local church wherever I have lived. In fact, I shudder to think what would have become of me over the years if I had not been a true part of the body. I was part of a home cell group in the 1970s when one of our group's members lost a child in an accidental drowning. When a person is in shock, he cannot even articulate his deepest needs. I saw firsthand how the body of Christ rallied around that family, meeting every need without being asked.

Of course, for this type of body ministry to be truly effective, the body must know the person, as our group did, so it can corporately swing into appropriate action.

I have surrendered two beloved wives to the Lord in death: Lydia in 1975 and Ruth in 1998. The grief through which I passed would be difficult to express, but the love of my brothers and sisters got me through those times. Anyone present at the memorial service for my wife Ruth will remember my first words, spoken through the tears that became very much a part of my life: "I am not crying because I am sad but because I never knew there was so much love in the world!" The messages of comfort and love from around the world, received from people I had never met, were an overwhelming blessing to me. Those with whom I walked daily simply rose up, took care of me, and walked me through those painful months. I could never have done it alone, and fortunately I did not have to.

I feel sad for those who rob themselves of "body life" through rebellion or independence. They are missing out on the love that God expresses organically through Christ's body. I would never have known fully the love of God had I not passed through grief in the arms of the body of Christ. Don't make the mistake that many have of finding themselves alone and without the resources of the body when they deeply need them. Don't say, "If tragedy comes my way, I can make it alone!" Once trouble begins, it is too late to start building relationships within the body. Find your place now and nurture close friendships with your fellow Christians. Not only do you need them, but they also need you!

5

PICTURE #3:
THE WORKMANSHIP

*"For we are His workmanship, created in Christ Jesus for good works,
which God prepared beforehand that we should walk in them."*
—Ephesians 2:10

We have taken a look at the first two pictures of what God intends His people to become: the assembly of God and the body of Christ. We have a serious role to play in the governmental assembly that exercises spiritual judgment and authority in the earth; and we flow together in unity, joined to our brothers and sisters as members of the same body. One function is *governmental*, the other is *relational*.

God's Creative Masterpiece

The third picture is *the workmanship*. The English translation of Ephesians 2:10 does not fully bring out the real significance of this picture. The Greek word translated *"workmanship"* is *poiema*. The Latin version is *poema*, from which we get the English word *poem*. The *Jerusalem Bible* uses the phrase *"work of art."* In other words, this word is taken from the field of art and creativity. I like to translate it as, "We are God's creative masterpiece," which more properly conveys Paul's meaning.

When you ponder all that God has created, it is breathtaking and humbling that God would choose people like us to be the materials for His creative masterpiece.

Think for a moment of what is involved in a creative work of art. For example, consider the art of sculpture. There are so many examples of beautiful sculpture in Greek antiquity. When the right tools are used with great skill and patience, the practical outworking follows the inner vision. The sculptor creatively envisions within a block of marble something to be revealed. He arms himself with a chisel and his inner mental vision of what he wants to produce, and he begins to chip away at the stone. Gradually, the form emerges, which is the expression of the artist's inner vision.

> *THE MORE YOU ALLOW GOD TO CUT AWAY, THE BETTER YOUR VISION IS REVEALED.*

When I was working with Elizabeth Sherrill on my wife Lydia's book, *Appointment in Jerusalem*, I produced the manuscript after two years of labor. Elizabeth said, "Now go through it and take out about 20 percent." If you have ever worked for two years on a book, you know what that means!

She quoted to me what Michelangelo said about his statues: "Every stroke of the chisel reveals a little bit more of the plan." The more you cut away, the better your vision is revealed. Likewise, as God goes on cutting and cutting and cutting, you might wonder, "Lord, is there going to be anything left of me?" But every stroke of His chisel reveals more perfectly the plan of the Master Artist.

We could also consider the art of painting. The essence of painting includes the blending of form and color in the right proportions to produce a scene or an object. The painter's blending of the shapes, colors, and forms can help us see aspects we may have missed when we looked at the actual scene or object. So it is with us. God works on us, blending and shaping and positioning us, and then He unveils us to the world, which is then able to see something in us it did not perceive before.

Consider another example of creative work, that of poetry. I have always been particularly interested in poetry. I have even written a few poems myself. In essence, poetry is artistry with words. It is the blending together of words to evoke a picture, make an impression, or create an impact. Each word must be the precise word set in just the right place and perfectly related to the words around it. In the same way, God wants to make us collectively into a poem, with each one of us being carefully selected and placed in the right position in relation to all the others around us.

We are God's poem, His creative masterpiece, *"to the intent that now the manifold wisdom of God might be made known by the church* [God's people] *to the principalities and powers in the heavenly places"* (Ephesians 3:10).

Paul's statement is astonishing. It is breathtaking to know that God chose us, His redeemed people, to demonstrate His manifold wisdom to the entire universe—in time and eternity—and to the unseen heavenly realms! The word *manifold* is a vivid word that I translate as "many-sided." Each one of us demonstrates a unique refraction of the overall, multifaceted wisdom of God, and we all blend into a harmonious whole!

Where did God go for the material to make this greatest creative masterpiece, His church? He went to the scrap heap! To the broken pieces of lives that had been marred by sin. To the pile of broken families, sick bodies, and corrupted minds.

In Ephesians 2:10, in a very beautiful, yet practical, way, Paul told us that we were created to do the good works that God prepared in advance for us to do. This verse tells us that we are not merely to be ornamental; we are also to be *useful.* We are to fulfill a function. We are not just to stand around and be interesting and spiritual. God has a good *work* for each believer to accomplish! Our assignment is to find those good works and to walk in them.

There is no room for improvisation. None of us is free to write the score for his own life—God has already written it. We find our place in that creative masterpiece when we yield to God. Then we discover something ready for us to do that we might never have dreamed. If someone had told me years ago that I would someday become a teacher of the Bible, I would have laughed. My friends would have laughed louder still because there was nothing in me at that time that gave the faintest indication of what God planned to make out of me.

The Essential Feature of Workmanship and God's Requirement

The essential feature of the picture of the masterpiece—the *poiema*—is the demonstration of *God's creative genius.* God has been a creator right from the beginning, and He's still creating today. He created the heavenly bodies, the stars, the seas, the mountains, the animals, and the flowers. And when He finished all that, He said, "My greatest masterpiece is still to come." *We* are that masterpiece—the ultimate revelation of God's creative genius!

Yieldedness

What is required of us as members of His *poiema* is summed up in one word: *yieldedness.* If we are a word in a poem, we just take our place. If we are a piece of clay in the Potter's hand, we just let Him mold us. If we are part of a block of marble, we just let Him chip away at us. We don't argue with Him or tell Him how to do His work. We don't ask, "God, do You really know what You're doing with me?" The key is yieldedness. As we willingly surrender ourselves fully into His hands, He will shape us into His marvelous work.

> But now, O LORD, You are our Father; we are the clay, and You our potter; and all we are the work of Your hand.   (Isaiah 64:8)

Once we put ourselves in God's hands, it is up to Him to make of us what He wants.

Merge-Ability

What does it require of us toward each other to fulfill this picture of God's creative masterpiece? I had to invent a word to describe our responsibility: merge-ability, the ability to merge with others. Other appropriate words might be blending or cohesiveness. What we are individually is not the most important thing; it is what we become together that is the final goal. For that, we must demonstrate a willingness to lose our individual identities to attain a greater whole.

When God wants to shape us, change us, and mold us, He uses pressure. When we are experiencing pressure, we want to say, "God, I can't stand it any longer!" Yet He says, "I'm doing it to make you not the way you want to be but the way I want you to be." All of us who love the Lord will experience the pressure of His hands in the days that lie ahead. The wheel is going to spin faster and faster. The pressure may grow more intense. But as long as we stay in His presence and remain pliable, we will emerge as the vessel He wants us to be.

> But indeed, O man, who are you to reply against God? Will the thing formed say to him who formed it, "Why have you made me like this?"
> (Romans 9:20)

Romans 9 is one of the more difficult theological chapters of the Bible because it deals with God's sovereign predestination. Paul talked about the potter making a vessel for "dishonor"—something that is unclean—and a vessel for "*honor*" (verse 21). Predestination says, in essence, that God determines what He will make out of every piece of material. He determines whether He will make a garbage can or a flower vase. We do not have the choice; it is God's decision. This is, of course, not the entire picture, which must be balanced by other truths. We do have free will. But, while we don't know exactly how our freedom to choose and predestination work hand in hand, God knows what choices we will make.

The apostle Paul wrote:

Does not the potter have power over the clay, from the same lump to make one vessel for honor and another for dishonor? What if God, wanting to show His wrath and to make His power known, endured with much longsuffering the vessels of wrath prepared for destruction, and that He might make known the riches of His glory on the vessels of mercy, which He had prepared beforehand for glory, even us whom He called, not of the Jews only, but also of the Gentiles?

(Romans 9:21–24)

God uses some vessels to show His wrath upon. The example Paul used in Romans 9 was Pharaoh. God said to Pharaoh, "*For this very purpose I have raised you up, that I may show My power in you*" (verse 17).

If you discover that you are a vessel of glory, you can say, "Praise the Lord; it's not my doing. It's His choice." For, "*it is not of him who wills, nor of him who runs, but of God who shows mercy*" (verse 16). As difficult as it may be for some to accept, we need to get back to that neglected part of God's truth.

The essence of this particular picture is that, in some ways, we are passive. The clay cannot give the orders or make the decisions. If this was the only picture of God's people, it would be incomplete. But our understanding of what it is to be God's people is also incomplete without this picture. Modern Western culture probably needs a much clearer vision of what it means to be willing clay in the hands of a loving Potter.

I have met many people who have never accepted themselves as God's workmanship or masterpiece. God cannot fully use you until you accept yourself as God has made you. Simply have faith that the best is yet to come! The most exciting developments within my ministry began when I was in my late fifties, after several decades of often obscure, exacting labor. I have always stayed true to the call God gave me long ago, through a message in tongues and its interpretation, to be "a teacher of the Scriptures in truth and faith and love, which are in Christ Jesus, for many." The "many" did not appear until much later in my life, but the ministry came to pass.

We are His workmanship, created for a significant task. We are important to His plan, and we must be confident concerning whom He is making us into!

6

PICTURE #4:
THE FAMILY

"For through Him we both have access by one Spirit to the Father.
Now, therefore, you are no longer strangers and foreigners, but fellow
citizens with the saints and members of the household of God
[or members of God's family]."
—Ephesians 2:18–19

As we continue looking by faith into the mirror of God's Word to find out what kind of people we are in His sight, God truly wants us to understand how central we are to the outworking of His purposes in the earth.

We now turn to the fourth picture taken from Paul's epistle to the Ephesians: the family. In this list of seven pictures of God's people, the fourth is in the center. I believe this is appropriate because the family is central to our understanding of God's people. In the New Testament, His people are very seldom referred to by the title Christians or even believers. The most common title used is brothers, emphasizing membership in one spiritual family.

> *For through Him we both* [Jews and Gentiles] *have access by one Spirit to the Father.* (Ephesians 2:18)

Notice again that all three persons of the Godhead are represented here: through Jesus the Son, we have access to the Father, by one Spirit. The next verse reveals the wondrous result:

> *Now, therefore* [because we have access to the Father], *you are no longer strangers and foreigners, but fellow citizens with the saints and members of the household of God.* (Ephesians 2:19)

The word *"household"* would be best represented in contemporary English by *family*. Because Christ has gained us access to the Father, we have become members of God's family.

Relationship to the Father

God's family is determined by relationship to the Father. In New Testament Greek, there is a very close similarity between the words *father* and *family*. The word for father is *pater*; the word for family is *patria*, which is derived from *pater*. This relationship is brought out clearly in Paul's prayer:

> *For this reason I bow my knees to the Father of our Lord Jesus Christ, from whom the whole family in heaven and earth is named.*
> (Ephesians 3:14–15)

There is a direct play here on the words *"Father"* and *"family."* From God the Father (*pater*) the whole family (*patria*) in heaven and earth is named. Family comes from fatherhood. So, again, having God as our Father makes us members of His family.

This truth is further brought out by the writer of Hebrews:

> For it was fitting for Him [God the Father], for whom are all things, and through whom are all things, in bringing many sons [believers] to glory, to perfect the author [the Lord Jesus] of their salvation through sufferings. For both He who sanctifies [Jesus] and those who are sanctified [the believers] are all from one Father; for which reason He [Jesus] is not ashamed to call them brethren, saying [quoting from the Old Testament], "I will proclaim Thy name to My brethren, in the midst of the congregation I will sing Thy praise."
>
> (Hebrews 2:10–12 NASB)

There is a beautiful revelation in this passage. God has made us His sons through Jesus, and Jesus Himself is the only begotten Son of God the Father; therefore, Jesus acknowledges us as His brothers because of our relationship to the Father. Jesus never did anything without the Father leading the way. Jesus did not call us "brothers" until the Father called us "sons." Once His Father called us sons, then He acknowledged us as His brothers.

ALWAYS APPROACH GOD AS YOUR LOVING HEAVENLY FATHER.

There are two main features of this particular revelation that emphasize the idea of fatherhood:

The primary, decisive feature is a shared life-source. When we all share the same life-source, we are members of the same family. The Father is the source of every family, heavenly or earthly. A family is not a denomination or a label, nor is it an organization or an institution. A family is a family because it has a shared life-source.

Second, God's fatherhood has relational implications in two directions: vertical and horizontal. The vertical is the relationship that each of us has to God as Father. The horizontal is the relationships we all have to one another as members of the same family. The vertical relationship to God is primary, but it also gives us a horizontal responsibility to one another. We cannot claim to be God's sons if we do not acknowledge His other sons as our brothers!

These two relationships, the vertical and the horizontal, within the family of God are beautifully exemplified by the opening words of the Lord's Prayer:

> *In this manner, therefore, pray: Our Father in heaven, hallowed be Your name.*   (Matthew 6:9)

Two very important words occur right at the beginning of this prayer: *"Our Father."* In the original Greek, it is actually "Father our." So the first word is *Father,* which is the decisive word. Jesus is saying, "Keep in mind that, through Me, you become children of God. Always approach God as your Father. Don't come to Him only as God, because He is God over everyone. Come to Him as your loving heavenly Father, with whom you are now in right relationship."

The second word is *our*—not "my" Father, but "our" Father. What does this mean? In coming to God as "our" Father, we acknowledge that He has many other children. You are not an only child. All of God's other children are your brothers and sisters. This acknowledgment rules out self-centeredness on our part.

There is so much in those two simple, introductory words to the Lord's Prayer.

In John 14, when Jesus was talking to the disciples about the Father, one of them said, *"Lord, show us the Father"* (verse 8). This grieved Jesus, and He said,

> *Have I been with you so long, and yet you have not known Me, Philip?*
> *He who has seen Me has seen the Father; so how can you say, "Show us*
> *the Father"?*   (John 14:9)

Just before that, in John 14:6, Jesus said, *"I am the way, the truth, and the life. No one comes to the Father except through Me."* People often quote that Scripture, but they very rarely complete it. Jesus said, *"I am the way"*; but a way is not an end in itself. A way is meaningless unless it leads us somewhere. Where does Jesus, the Way, lead us? To the Father! We have not fulfilled the purpose of God if we merely find the way. What we have to find is *the end* of the way! The primary mission of Jesus Christ is not to bring us to Himself but to bring us to the Father.

> *For Christ also suffered once for sins, the just for the unjust, that He*
> *might bring us to God.*   (1 Peter 3:18)

God's purpose is to gather in a great family of sons patterned after the pattern Son, Jesus. Everything is working together for good along the line of that purpose, to make us sons conformed to the image of Jesus Christ.

> *And we know that all things work together for good to those who love*
> *God, to those who are the called according to His purpose. For whom*
> *He foreknew, He also predestined to be conformed to the image of His*
> *Son, that [the Son] might be the firstborn among many brethren.*
>   (Romans 8:28–29)

The Central Concept of the Family Is Obedience

The central concept that these passages evoke concerning our relationship to God as our Father is *obedience*.

For it was fitting for Him, for whom are all things and by whom are all things, in bringing many sons to glory, to make the captain of their salvation perfect through sufferings. (Hebrews 2:10)

The *"Him"* spoken of in this passage is God the Father; the *"captain"* of our salvation is Jesus; and the *"many sons"* are we, the believers.

The writer of Hebrews told us that the captain of our salvation was made perfect through sufferings. Jesus was morally perfect, but in personal development He wasn't perfect until God brought Him to maturity. He grew up as the pattern Son under the discipline and discipleship of the Father, who brought Him to full personal development. He then became the pattern for all sons on their way to maturity. Again, the process through which He was perfected was suffering.

For both He who sanctifies and those who are being sanctified are all of one, for which reason He is not ashamed to call them brethren. (Hebrews 2:11)

Jesus is *"He who sanctifies,"* and we are *"those who are being sanctified."* The *"one"* from whom Jesus and we proceed is the Father, from whom we receive our sanctification. Because we each go through the process of sanctification and maturity, we are given the right to our place in the family of God.

Quoting from Psalm 22, the passage continues,

He is not ashamed to call them brethren, saying: "I will declare Your name to My brethren; in the midst of the assembly I will sing praise to You." (Hebrews 2:11–12)

It is exciting to note that Jesus is going to sing in the midst of the church!

There is to be an unfolding revelation of God the Father to His children in the church through His Son Jesus. The revelation of God's fatherhood is what will bring the children to maturity even as they are perfected through suffering.

Though He was a Son, yet He learned obedience by the things which
He suffered.   (Hebrews 5:8)

The relationship between the Father and the Son is a study of the relationship of a father bringing a son into maturity. Thus, Jesus became the pattern and the pathway for us. Jesus was never disobedient. Yet He had to *learn* obedience. You and I have to learn it in the same way He did: by obeying! There is just no other way. We don't find out what obedience is by sitting and listening to sermons on obedience. These sermons may help us or motivate us, but obedience is learned by *doing*.

The key phrase in the obedience of Jesus was, *"Not My will, but Yours, be done"* (Luke 22:42). Every step of obedience in the Christian life is a step of self-denial. Jesus said if anyone desires to come after Him, he must deny himself. (See Matthew 16:24.) This is always painful because our ego never likes to be denied. The ego wants things, and following the Lord is a continual denial of ego.

Our Responsibility to Our Fellow Believers Is Love

While our vertical relationship to God can be characterized in this context as obedience, our horizontal responsibility to our brothers and sisters is a special kind of love. There are various Greek words that all tend to be translated as "love." Four of them are *eros* (sexual passion), *storgé* (natural family affection), *philadelphia* (brotherly love), and *agape* (divine love).

Love is not a spiritual gift but the outworking of *character*. In 2 Peter we see seven progressive steps that bring us to this special kind of *agape* love:

But also for this very reason, giving all diligence, add to your faith
virtue, to virtue knowledge, to knowledge self-control, to self-control
perseverance, to perseverance godliness, to godliness brotherly kindness,
and to brotherly kindness love [agape].   (2 Peter 1:5–7)

The Scripture says, *"Add to your faith...."* So, we start with the basis of faith, and then we add the seven things to that in succession:

1. Virtue (excellence)

2. Knowledge (knowing God's will)

3. Self-control (temperance)

4. Perseverance (patience, endurance)

5. Godliness (holiness)

We have come a long way down the list, but we have not yet come to love. The attitude that love means merely giving somebody an embrace at a prayer meeting is not in line with Scripture. Love is something that has to be cultivated and achieved, and it is really high up the ladder. Then,

6. Brotherly kindness (goodwill toward men)

7. Love (*agape*)

The word *agape* means, in particular, "I love my enemies." When you can love your enemies, you have made it to the top.

Many religions have martyrs who will die for their faith—Judaism, Communism, and Islam, to name but a few. But there is one difference about the genuine Christian martyr in that he loves his enemies. If he does not, he is no better than the Communist or Muslim martyr.

Most of us are not qualified to be martyrs; God could not give us that privilege. I am convinced that if you are going to be a real martyr, you have to train for it by laying down your life daily. A martyr does not become one by a sudden, dramatic accident but as the result of a process.

I have learned that every time I minister fruitfully, it is due to self-denial. As long as I am pleasing myself, I am not ministering the life of Christ. The two are opposites. Christ's life flows only where self has been denied. Jesus said we are to take up our cross daily. Your cross is the place where your will and God's will *cross*—and you have to come to that place of surrender on a daily basis. A person can be very religious, yet never die to his own will.

Many Christians have not even achieved "brotherly kindness." It is not always easy to love every one of our fellow Christians. Sometimes, it is easier to love nonbelievers than Christians because it doesn't matter to them whether you are baptized by immersion or sprinkling or if you raise your hands in prayer or not.

THE FATHER IS THE SOURCE OF EVERY FAMILY, HEAVENLY OR EARTHLY.

I recall an incident in my life when I was involved in some meetings with about thirty other leaders. We were to be paired together with a different leader each night at a different meeting. There was one brother with whom I totally disagreed about baptism. I said to myself, *I just hope I don't get put together with him!* And, you guessed it—I was put together with him for three nights. He and I are now close friends.

In conclusion, let me relate a little incident from the days when some of the Scottish Christians up in the Highlands were being severely persecuted by the English army. As a Scottish lassie was on her way to a secret meeting of believers, she was arrested by an English policeman who asked her where she was going. She did not want to lie, but she did not want to betray her fellow believers, either, so she lifted her heart to the Lord in prayer and asked Him for an answer. This is what she said to the policeman: "My Older Brother died, and I'm on my way to my Father's house to hear the will read." What a good answer! Jesus is the Elder Brother, God is our Father, and it is our Father's house. We are a family!

Again, the essential feature of this picture of family is our shared life-source. God our Father in heaven is the life-source of His entire family. We all share a common life. This is what binds us together—not denominations or doctrines or labels.

We need to accept one another as brothers and sisters because God has accepted us as His family. It is one thing to know that we are accepted by God, but quite another to know experientially the acceptance of our brethren. Some of us have never known the warm, loving embrace of an earthly father or brother. May these ones be destined to find it for the very first time in the family of God!

7

PICTURE #5: THE TEMPLE

"Jesus Christ Himself [is] *the chief corner stone, in whom the whole building, being joined together, grows into a holy temple in the Lord."*
—Ephesians 2:20–21

We now come to the fifth picture, that of the building or *the temple.* Let's begin by reviewing Paul's statement in Ephesians in connection with the family.

> *Now, therefore, you are no longer strangers and foreigners, but fellow citizens with the saints and members of the household of God* [or members of God's family].... (Ephesians 2:19)

Paul then moved from the picture of the family to the picture of the temple:

> *...having been built on the foundation of the apostles and prophets, Jesus Christ Himself being the chief corner stone, in whom the whole building, being joined together, grows into a holy temple in the Lord, in whom you also are being built together for a dwelling place of God in the Spirit.* (Ephesians 2:20–22)

The Christians—the true believers—are the people in whom God dwells and moves. Because of this relationship, He is their God and they are His people.

> *...in whom the whole building, being fitted together, grows into a holy temple in the Lord, in whom [Jesus] you also are being built together for a dwelling place of God in the Spirit.* (Ephesians 2:21–22)

Notice that all three persons of the Godhead are involved once again. The Father indwells those who are in the Son by the Spirit. The end purpose of the church here is to be a habitation, a dwelling place of God.

THE END PURPOSE OF THE CHURCH IS TO BE A HABITATION, A DWELLING PLACE OF GOD.

In Hebrew, the word for a house (*beit*), which includes the concept of a home or family, is directly connected with the word "to build." So there is a close connection, in Hebrew thought, between a family and a building. In fact, the word *house* was used in Hebrew not to describe a physical dwelling but rather a family of people. Those two thoughts always go together. Notice the emphasis on building in this passage: "*built*," "*building*," "temple," "built," "dwelling place." Five times, the thought is brought out in those verses.

The principle is this: God has always required His people to provide Him with a dwelling place. When God delivered the Israelites out of Egypt, brought them to Mt. Sinai, and gave them His first covenant, one of the first things He required of them was that they build Him a tabernacle. This tent was the dwelling place of His manifest presence—His shekinah glory—and it traveled with Israel all the way through the wilderness.

After God brought the Israelites into the promised land, He gave them instructions to build a temple for Him in a certain city of His choice—Jerusalem. Solomon constructed the most glorious, costly, and elaborate edifice that has ever been built by humanity. Through Israel's idolatry and disobedience, however, this temple was eventually destroyed by the Babylonians under Nebuchadnezzar. But again, after God in His mercy granted Israel a restoration from Babylon, one of their first assignments was to build Him another temple.

It is very interesting to note that God did not leave the decision about the dwelling place to His people; He determined it Himself—the location, the types of materials, and the shape of the structure. However, the Bible also makes it clear that these buildings (the tabernacle and the two temples) were only patterns of something infinitely more valuable and important. This idea is brought out very clearly by the words of Stephen to the Jewish council:

> However, the Most High [the true God] does not dwell in temples made with hands, as the prophet says: "Heaven is My throne, and earth is My footstool. What house will you build for Me? says the LORD, or what is the place of My rest? Has My hand not made all these things?" (Acts 7:48–50)

The Material of the Temple

Any material building constructed by men, no matter how wonderful it may be, is not the final dwelling place of God. It is just a temporary place that He honors with His presence as long as His people meet His conditions. The final, eternal temple of God, the one that all others are just a preview and a pattern of, is made up of *people*. People are the most valuable creatures in the universe. The temple of God obviously has to be made of the most valuable material—not gold or silver or marble, but people. This truth is clearly brought out in various passages of the New Testament:

> *According to the grace of God which was given to me, as a wise master builder [apostle] I have laid the foundation, and another builds on it. But let each one take heed how he builds on it. For no other foundation can anyone lay than that which is laid, which is Jesus Christ. Now if anyone builds on this foundation with gold, silver, precious stones, wood, hay, straw....* (1 Corinthians 3:10–12)

There are two kinds of buildings you can erect: those that will stand the test and those that will not. You can build in great quantity with wood, hay, and stubble; there is no difficulty in obtaining those materials in large quantities, but they will not stand the test. Or you can build in much smaller quantities with much more precious materials, and they will stand the test.

> *...each one's work will become clear; for the Day will declare it, because it will be revealed by fire; and the fire will test each one's work, of what sort it is. If anyone's work which he has built on it endures, he will receive a reward. If anyone's work is burned, he will suffer loss; but he himself will be saved, yet so as through fire.* (verses 13–15)

This Scripture is talking about our contribution in the service of God's house; it is going to have to stand the test of fire.

> *For we must all appear before the judgment seat of Christ, that each one may receive the things done in the body, according to what he has done, whether good or bad.* (2 Corinthians 5:10)

Every Christian is going to appear before the judgment seat of Christ to be judged for all the service that he or she has offered God in His house. This is not a judgment of salvation or condemnation, for there is no condemnation for those who are in Christ Jesus. (See Romans 8:1.) It will not be concerning the destiny of our souls, but it will be concerning the work that we have done in the house of God. Every man's work will be tried by fire. If it stands the test, he will receive a reward; if it is burned up, he will lose his reward, but his soul will still be saved.

The prize-giving has not yet come; it lies ahead. It behooves each one of us to ask what type of material we are putting into the building. Will it stand the test of fire? Paul said to the leaders in Corinth:

Do you not know that you are the temple of God and that the Spirit of God dwells in you? If anyone defiles the temple of God, God will destroy him. For the temple of God is holy, which temple you are.
(1 Corinthians 3:16–17)

It seems that the Corinthian believers were somewhat ignorant of what they really were intended to be. This, again, is one of the important reasons for looking in the mirror of God's Word: to see what we really are! Paul rebuked them, "Don't you know that you're God's temple? You'd better be careful how you live."

Keeping the Temple Pure

In connection with the temple, there is always a warning against defiling it—both the collective temple and the individual temple.

We have looked at the collective temple, which is all believers united together. Now let's look at the individual temple:

Or do you not know that your body is the temple of the Holy Spirit who is in you, whom you have from God, and you are not your own? For you were bought at a price; therefore glorify God in your body and in your spirit, which are God's.
(1 Corinthians 6:19–20)

Every believer has the privilege of providing his physical body to the Holy Spirit as a temple to dwell in. God, through Jesus Christ, redeemed your body so that it might be a temple for His Spirit. Notice again that we are warned to be careful that we do not defile or destroy the temple. Whether it is the collective temple or the individual temple, we are required to take care of it and to preserve it in purity, in health, and in holiness because it is the temple of the Holy Spirit. We are obligated to provide Him with a temple that honors Him and serves His purpose. I personally believe that the care of our physical bodies is much more important in the sight of God than most of us recognize it to be.

> *Do not be unequally yoked together with unbelievers. For what fellow-ship has righteousness with lawlessness? And what communion has light with darkness? And what accord has Christ with Belial [Satan]? Or what part has a believer with an unbeliever? And what agreement has the temple of God with idols? For you are the temple of the living God. As God has said: "I will dwell in them and walk among them ["walk in them" KJV]. I will be their God, and they shall be My people."*
> (2 Corinthians 6:14–16)

Notice again that it is the collective temple we are talking about here. This is the conviction upon which God becomes our God, that He is allowed to dwell in us and walk in us. I like the phrase *"walk in them"* from the King James Version. It indicates that God has a mobile temple that is not confined to one place. Wherever we are, God is; He goes where we go. As His body, we provide Him with an instrument; but as a temple, we provide Him with a dwelling place. In this sense, it is not really accurate to talk about going to church, as though there is a certain place where we meet God. Instead, where we come together, there is where the church is. And where the church is, God is. If we go to the seashore, the church goes to the seashore. If the church goes to the seashore, God goes to the seashore. He dwells in us and walks in us, and on that condition He is our God and we are His people.

Living Stones

> *Coming to [Jesus] as to a living stone, rejected indeed by men, but chosen by God and precious, you also, as living stones, are being built up a spiritual house, a holy priesthood.* (1 Peter 2:4–5)

In this spiritual house that God is building for His eternal dwelling place, you and I and all our fellow believers together are *"living stones"*! We are being built together to constitute the final, eternal house that God has destined from eternity, of which all His previous dwelling places in the Old Testament were but previews and patterns.

WE ARE "LIVING STONES" IN GOD'S ETERNAL, SPIRITUAL HOUSE.

I have spent a number of years of my life in Jerusalem, where the only material permitted for building is stone. This has greatly helped to preserve the unique character and beauty of Jerusalem. All permitted buildings in Jerusalem are built out of stone from a quarry somewhere to the north. In the 1940s, I lived in a town north of Jerusalem, and I used to pass the place where they quarried the stones and then carried them into Jerusalem. I remember seeing a stone that had fallen off the truck on its way into the city and was just left by the roadside. Nobody picked it up; it was just left there. I thought to myself, "That stone lies there in its individual, egotistic self-will. No chisel will ever be applied to that stone. It'll stay just the way it is—but it will never get into the building." Believers like that have been quarried out, but they have never been built in. They are not finding their places in God's purposes.

Note what 1 Kings has to say about the temple of Solomon:

And the temple, when it was being built, was built with stone finished at the quarry, so that no hammer or chisel or any iron tool was heard in the temple while it was being built.   (1 Kings 6:7)

That is remarkable! The dimensions for every stone were predetermined, and every stone was shaped and cut into its predetermined dimensions at the quarry. There was no last-minute hammering or chiseling in the actual structure of the temple.

God is doing the same for you and me. He quarries us out of this world by the gospel, and then He proceeds to shape us, so that when the final edifice rises, there will be no more hammering and chiseling. We have to be ready to be shaped now, a process that we all must undergo if we are going to take our part in that temple.

The Essential Feature of the Temple and God's Requirement

Let's look now at the twofold application of the temple. The essential feature of this picture of the church is that the temple is *God's dwelling place*. It is where God is going to reside forever. We always tend to think about getting to heaven, but the ultimate purpose of God is to get heaven to earth! The last picture in the Bible of God's people, found in Revelation 21:1–4, is of a beautiful dwelling place coming down out of heaven to earth. Study that passage about the New Jerusalem sometime; it is a glorious picture of God's dwelling coming to earth.

What is required of us? We are to be willing to be quarried out, shaped, and chiseled; we are to have our edges knocked off, to fit in with a predetermined dimension, and to be made ready before the final structure arises. This is a huge commitment on our part, but one that brings an eternal reward!

After reminding the believers that they are the *"temple of the living God"* (2 Corinthians 6:16), Paul made reference to several Old Testament passages, saying,

> Therefore *"Come out from among them and be separate, says the Lord. Do not touch what is unclean, and I will receive you. I will be a **Father** to you, and you shall be My **sons and daughters**, says the* LORD *Almighty."* (2 Corinthians 6:17–18, emphasis added)

Notice how close the picture of the family and the picture of the temple are, which we have previously seen in Ephesians 2:19–22. The temple and the family are united. God is the Father of His family, and He is the God who dwells in His temple.

Once again, the lesson is pressed home regarding God's requirement of holiness, for the next chapter begins with these words:

Therefore, having these promises, beloved, let us cleanse ourselves from all filthiness of the flesh and spirit, perfecting holiness in the fear of God.   (2 Corinthians 7:1)

This is something that we have to do: cleanse ourselves from all filthiness of flesh and spirit. I believe *"filthiness of the flesh"* is immorality, drunkenness, and so on, and *"filthiness of the...spirit"* is essentially occult involvement. We are to perfect holiness in the fear of God. The message is one that emphasizes the need for purity and for care in our attitude toward the temple.

My personal attitude in this regard is that I desire never to be a cause of harm to a family or a church. I think they are the two most sacred things on earth. It is my sincere desire and prayer that I will never offend one or the other. If you touch the work of God, remember, you are going to have to answer to Him.

8

PICTURE #6:
THE BRIDE

*"Christ also loved the church and gave Himself for her, that He might
sanctify and cleanse her with the washing of water by the word, that
He might present her to Himself a glorious church,
not having spot or wrinkle or any such thing, but that she should be
holy and without blemish."*
—Ephesians 5:25–27

We turn now to the sixth picture, the bride. Although the word *bride* is not actually used in Ephesians, the concept is specifically stated in other passages of the Bible, and it is implied in this passage:

Husbands, love your wives, just as Christ also loved the church and gave Himself for her, that He might sanctify and cleanse her with the washing of water by the word, that He might present her to Himself a glorious church, not having spot or wrinkle or any such thing, but that she should be holy and without blemish. So husbands ought to love their own wives as their own bodies; he who loves his wife loves himself. For no one ever hated his own flesh, but nourishes and cherishes it, just as the Lord does the church. For we are members of His body, of His flesh and of His bones. "For this reason a man shall leave his father and mother and be joined to his wife, and the two shall become one flesh." This is a great mystery, but I speak concerning Christ and the church.

(Ephesians 5:25–32)

Paul began by speaking to believing husbands about their relationship to their wives. He said the relationship must be one of love, devotion, and care—all very sound and practical advice, and much needed today. Yet this is not the full meaning of the passage, because Paul then went on to say that the husband/wife relationship is patterned on the relationship of Christ to His church, and he added, "*This is a great* [or profound] *mystery.*" It is, indeed. I am sure no human mind can ever fully fathom that mystery. But he said very clearly, "*I speak concerning Christ and the church.*" Thus, we see with absolute clarity the two persons in this union: Christ is the Bridegroom and the church is His bride.

HUMAN HISTORY BEGAN WITH A MARRIAGE AND WILL END WITH A MARRIAGE.

This relationship was very beautifully foreshadowed in the original creation of Adam and Eve as recorded in the opening chapters of Genesis.

One of the remarkable features of the creation of Adam was that God had everything ready for him before he appeared on the scene. His entire environment was there: the vegetation, the animals, the weather, and the heavenly bodies—everything he would need.

This is a wonderful picture of God's provision for us in the new creation. Everything we need is already there when we arrive on the scene. There was just one thing missing for Adam: a mate. This was not a mistake on God's part. God had a purpose in not immediately providing a mate for Adam, for He wanted Adam to understand something of the longing that He has for personal fellowship with human beings. So He allowed Adam to experience the lack of that fellowship, the lack of a mate. He then provided a mate, as recorded in Genesis:

> The LORD God said, "It is not good for the man to be alone. I will make a helper suitable for him."... So the LORD God caused the man to fall into a deep sleep; and while he was sleeping, he took one of the man's ribs and closed up the place with flesh. Then the LORD God made a woman from the rib he had taken out of the man, and he brought her to the man. The man said, "This is now bone of my bones and flesh of my flesh; she shall be called 'woman,' for she was taken out of man."
> (Genesis 2:18, 21–23 NIV)

The Bible puts tremendous emphasis on marriage. We need to fully appreciate how central a place marriage plays in Scripture. Human history began with a marriage—and the first matchmaker was God. God is still in the matchmaking business! One day, just as God presented Eve to Adam, He is going to present the church to Jesus at the marriage supper of the Lamb. (See Revelation 21:2–3, 9–11.) Let's look more closely at the circumstances of this spiritual marriage.

Making Ourselves Ready

Human history will come to a glorious climax with the marriage of the church, the bride, to Jesus Christ, the Bridegroom:

And I heard, as it were, the voice of a great multitude and as the sound of many waters and as the sound of mighty peals of thunder, saying, "Hallelujah! For the Lord our God, the Almighty, reigns. Let us rejoice and be glad and give the glory to Him [here is one primary cause for rejoicing], for the marriage of the Lamb [Jesus] has come and His bride has made herself ready." And it was given to her to clothe herself in fine linen, bright and clean; for the fine linen is the righteous acts of the saints. (Revelation 19:6–8 NASB)

The marriage of the church to Jesus Christ will be a cause for rejoicing throughout the universe.

It is interesting to note that the bride was expected to provide or prepare her own clothing. In the Bible, "fine linen" is always a type of purity. In one place in Ezekiel, priests who were girded with wool were not permitted access to the presence of the Lord. (See Ezekiel 44:15–18.) There had to be absolute purity in the priesthood. In Deuteronomy 22:11, the Israelites were instructed not to wear garments of mixed material, such as wool and linen. So, here, *"fine linen"* speaks of absolute purity. And it says the fine linen is *"the righteous acts of the saints"* or *"the righteousness of saints"* (KJV).

There are two Greek words for righteousness: one is *dikaiosune* and the other is *dikaioma. Dikaiosune* is righteousness in the abstract; *dikaioma* is righteousness in action. When you and I believe in Jesus Christ, His righteousness, *dikaiosune*, is imputed to us—we are made righteous with His righteousness. When we live out our faith, we express that imputed righteousness in *dikaioma*, which is outworked righteousness or our acts of righteousness.

Interestingly, the word used here is *dikaioma*, or the plural, *dikaiomata*. The fine linen is the righteous acts of the saints. That is a very searching statement. *"His bride has made herself ready."* How? By her righteous acts.

In every culture that I have ever known, there is one rule about marriage. The bridegroom never prepares the bride; the bride always prepares herself. The responsibility is placed on her. The Scripture says that Jesus Christ's bride has made herself ready by her outworked, righteous acts. The imputed righteousness of Christ will not avail for the bridal feast. It has to be the outworked righteousness.

Years ago, in Jerusalem, my wife and I had a missionary friend whom we knew well and who had become sick. She lay sick for a long while, and she thought she was going to die. One night, the Lord gave her a vivid dream. In this dream, she was working on a beautiful white dress. As she looked at the dress, she saw that much of it was not yet finished; there was a lot more work to do on it. When she woke up in the morning, she realized the Lord had shown her that she was not ready to go home because her work was not yet finished. I always think about this incident when I hear the verse, *"The marriage of the Lamb has come, and His wife has made herself ready."* Every one of us has wedding attire to complete, and we complete it by our acts of obedience. This is very important.

There is a parallel passage about outworked righteousness in Philippians:

> *Therefore, my beloved, as you have always obeyed, not as in my presence only, but now much more in my absence, work out your own salvation with fear and trembling; for it is God who works in you both to will and to do for His good pleasure.* (Philippians 2:12–13)

There is a balance there. God works in you, first *"to will,"* and then *"to do,"* God's pleasure. The Christian life is not about struggling to do something against our wills that we do not want to do. Rather, God works in us the will to do what He wants. Then He works in us the ability to do it.

God works *in* us only insofar as we work *out* what He works *in*. The measure of what God can work *in* is determined by the measure of what we work *out*. So there is a two-way process. God is working into us; but, by the way we live (our righteous acts), we are working out what God has worked in. This is the preparation of the bride. The fine linen is the righteous acts of the saints, so make sure you have the proper attire.

The Relationship between Bridegroom and Bride

I see three main elements in this picture of Christ as the Bridegroom and the church as the bride.

MUTUAL, UNRESERVED COMMITMENT

First of all, there is *mutual, unreserved commitment* on both sides. Jesus gave Himself up for the church, holding nothing back. He poured out His entire lifeblood. That is what marriage is, too. Even on the human level, God intends it to be a total self-giving of two people, the one to the other. Neither is entitled to hold anything back. It is required of the church that she give herself to Jesus, the Bridegroom, just as fully and totally as He gave Himself up to redeem her on the cross.

CAREFUL PREPARATION

The second step is *careful preparation*. We saw that the bride, the church, had made herself ready. She had prepared her attire, consisting of righteous acts. One single provision was not sufficient for everything, but her attire was continually being prepared. I like to think of life in the same way. As you and I walk in faith and obedience, fulfilling the will of God and keeping His commandments, we are preparing our attire—that fine linen that is bright and clean.

UNION THAT PRODUCES FRUIT

The third feature I see in this picture is *union that produces fruit*. The purpose and consummation of marriage is the union of two people. "*The two,*" it says, "*shall become one flesh*" (Matthew 19:5). Out of that union comes forth fruit—new life. I believe that is the purpose of God in the relationship of Christ, the Bridegroom, to the church, the bride. I believe that out of that glorious union, not yet consummated, will come eternal fruit. The eternal purposes of God for all subsequent ages will be unfolded out of the union of Christ with His church.

The Essential Feature of the Bride

Let us look at two verses in 1 Corinthians that tell us the essential feature of the bride is to reveal Christ's glory.

But I want you to know that the head of every man is Christ, the head of woman is man, and the head of Christ is God.

(1 Corinthians 11:3)

In descending order, God the Father is the head of Christ, Christ is the head of the man or the husband, and the husband is the head of the woman or the wife. There is a divine order of headship that starts in heaven and moves down into every home. This involves responsibilities on both sides.

For a man indeed ought not to cover his head, since he is the image and glory of God; but woman is the glory of man. (verse 7)

It was the male who was first created in the image and likeness of God to show forth God's likeness and glory to the rest of the creation. The wife was also made in the image of God, but her responsibility is to reflect her husband's glory. Likewise, as the bride of Christ, it is our responsibility to reflect His glory.

This is a very deep and practical teaching. I want to relate it to the marriage relationship because it is so close to that between Christ and His bride. Some women have the idea that because the Bible teaches the wife to be in submission to her husband, it implies inferiority. This is not so. Submission is not inferiority because Christ is in submission to the Father, but He is not inferior to the Father. In fact, He said, *"I and My Father are one"* (John 10:30). Submission is not inferiority but placement; it is being where you ought to be.

There are responsibilities between husband and wife. When I say that my wife is my glory, I am not really placing the responsibility so much on my wife as I am on myself. It is a very challenging responsibility. Somebody once asked a well-known preacher, "What kind of a Christian is Mr. Smith?" The preacher answered, "I can't tell you; I haven't met his wife!"

That is a very wise answer. If you want to know what kind of Christian Mr. Smith is, look at Mrs. Smith. She is his glory. As such, she reveals what he is really like. This challenges the husband much more than it does the wife. If you want to know what kind of Christian I am, you have to look at my wife. If my wife is restful, secure, joyful, fruitful, and relaxed, she is my glory. But if she is insecure, frustrated, and bitter, it tells you a lot about me. She is not my glory. It is my business to protect her. Ephesians 5:23 says, "[Christ] *is the Savior of the body,*" which is the church.

The problems in marriages that we see today began when the first man failed to protect his wife. You have to get behind the surface of the account in Genesis, but it is there. God placed Adam in the garden to *"tend and keep it"* (Genesis 2:15). The Hebrew word for *"keep"* means to protect it. He failed by letting the snake in. He ought never to have let the snake in because it was one of the beasts of the field; it had no place in the garden. Then Eve failed because she was away from her husband and met the snake in her own strength and wisdom, which she was not expected to do. Both of them were out of divine order. Surely, this tells us that the remedy for our problems is divine order.

THE BRIDE OF CHRIST, HIS CHURCH, IS TO REFLECT AND MANIFEST THE GLORY OF THE BRIDEGROOM.

The wife reflects what her husband is, and children reflect what their parents are. As a visiting preacher, I have discovered that a married couple can conceal their real attitudes toward me, but their children rarely do. If I go into a home where the children show me love and respect, I know that is what their parents feel. But when the children are undisciplined and disrespectful, the parents may talk nice to me, but I question whether that is their real attitude. We are always revealing ourselves in those to whom we are related.

God is present everywhere, but His *glory* is where His presence is manifested—where it can been seen and experienced. Many of us know what it is to feel the glory of God in our bodies or in the atmosphere, or to see it on the faces of other Christians. And the purpose of God in the church is to manifest the glory of Christ, the Bridegroom, in the church, the bride. Jesus is not coming for a spiritually bent, haggard, worn out, old crone of a bride. Please do not misunderstand me. I am not in any way speaking disrespectfully of old age. I am just pointing out that the bride Christ is coming for is going to glorify Him.

> *That we who first trusted in Christ should be to the praise of His glory.* (Ephesians 1:12)

We are to be the demonstration of His glory so that all the universe will praise His glory when they see it in us.

Let's return to our main Scripture in this chapter:

> *Husbands, love your wives, just as Christ also loved the church and gave Himself for her, that He might sanctify and cleanse her with the washing of water by the word....* (Ephesians 5:25–26)

I believe that this sanctifying and cleansing is what Christ is doing right now. The Greek word for *word* in this Scripture is *rhema*, which means the spoken word. One of the things that God does with a spoken teaching is to cleanse and sanctify the believers through the word that goes forth. Christ redeemed the church by His blood so that He might thereafter sanctify it by His word. Christ came by water and by blood. (See 1 John 6.) As the Redeemer, He came by blood, and as the Sanctifier, He came by water. He redeems the church by His blood; He sanctifies it by the water of His spoken word. It is only after the church has been sanctified that it will be what He intends it to be, which is described in the next verse:

...that He might present her to Himself a glorious church, not having spot or wrinkle or any such thing, but that she should be holy and without blemish.   (Ephesians 5:27)

This means that the church will be permeated with the manifest presence of God.

When you see a young woman who is really in love with her husband, her face just beams love at him. She is radiant. That is how God wants the church to be—a radiant church, without spot or wrinkle, unbelievably beautiful. Isn't it good that God can do it? And He *is* going to do it!

Our Requirement as the Bride

What is required in our relationship to Christ, the Bridegroom, as His bride? We can learn this by reading what Paul wrote to the church at Corinth, which was the product of his ministry:

For I am jealous for you with godly jealousy. For I have betrothed you to one husband, that I may present you as a chaste virgin to Christ. But I fear, lest somehow, as the serpent deceived Eve by his craftiness, so your minds may be corrupted from the simplicity that is in Christ. For if he who comes preaches another Jesus whom we have not preached, or if you receive a different spirit which you have not received, or a different gospel which you have not accepted; you may well put up with it!
                                                                (2 Corinthians 11:2–4)

Loyalty to Jesus

To understand this picture, it helps to be acquainted with the basic principles of marriage among the Jewish people, in which there were two main ceremonies. The first was betrothal, which is something like an engagement. The second, which usually followed about a year later, was the actual marriage ceremony and was followed by the physical union between the man and his bride. In Hebrew custom, betrothal was a very sacred, binding covenant agreement between a man and a woman. Although they still lived apart and did not come together in physical relationship, the woman was bound to the man by that covenant. If, in the course of that time, she broke her engagement to marry someone else or had sexual relations with another man, she was treated as an adulteress, and the covenant was officially nullified by something that was known as a divorce. That is how solemn the betrothal commitment was.

This practice is exemplified in the story of Joseph and Mary. They were betrothed, but not yet married, when Joseph discovered that Mary was pregnant. He did not yet know that this conception was by the Holy Spirit, in God's plan to bring His Son into the world, and the Scripture tells us that Joseph *"was minded to put her away secretly"* (Matthew 1:19), or divorce her.

OUR LOYALTY TO CHRIST WILL BE TESTED DURING OUR "ENGAGEMENT" PERIOD HERE ON EARTH.

In a similar way, when we become Christians, we are engaged to Christ, but the marriage has not yet taken place—that is still in the future. In this period between engagement and marriage, our loyalty to Christ is being tested. Paul was saying, "I want you to be a chaste virgin when you marry the Bridegroom."

There are some very beautiful thoughts in that statement because if any group of people, by natural standards, did not qualify to be a chaste virgin, it was the Corinthian Christians. They were prostitutes, homosexuals, and drunkards. Yet the grace and blood of Jesus gave them the privilege of being redeemed and cleansed, and therefore, in God's sight, of being a chaste virgin. It was as if they had never sinned. (See Isaiah 1:18; Romans 4:3–8.)

Nevertheless, Paul said to be careful not to lose your virginity. Be careful that you do not get tricked into a wrong relationship that will make you unfit to be the bride. This is so highly relevant to our contemporary situation.

> *But I fear, lest somehow, as the serpent deceived Eve by his craftiness, so your minds may be corrupted from the simplicity that is in Christ.*
>
> (2 Corinthians 11:3)

Paul was afraid for these Christians that the devil would get at their minds and corrupt them from the pure simplicity of faith in Jesus Christ and total commitment to Him. In the next verse, he described the way this could happen. Indeed, don't we see this happening all around us in the churches of America today?

> *For if he who comes preaches another Jesus whom we have not preached....*   (verse 4)

What kind of "other Jesus" was he referring to? Perhaps Jesus as a great teacher or the greatest guru, just a little higher than Buddha or Socrates or Plato or Martin Luther King Jr.—but not as a redeeming Savior. Or maybe a Jesus who was not born of a virgin? Or who is not truly divine? Those would be examples of *"another Jesus"* and exactly what Paul was talking about.

Then Paul said, *"If you receive a different spirit..."* (verse 4). These were Spirit-baptized Christians he was addressing. Was it possible for them to receive a different spirit? Apparently. How? Through receiving a wrong picture of Jesus. In other words, they might open their minds to an error that would, in turn, open their spirits to a spirit of error.

Paul went on, *"If you receive...a different gospel..."* (2 Corinthians 11:4). This could be a gospel that speaks only about the love of God and never about the judgment of God. Or a gospel that claims the fatherhood of God even over the unconverted. But the Bible does not say that the unconverted are the children of God; it says they are the children of the devil. All these things are happening today because the devil is seeking to corrupt the bride from her loyalty to Jesus Christ.

At the close of this age, it is my firm conviction that there will be only two groups in Christendom—not two denominations but two groups. One will be the bride and the other will be the harlot. What will the difference be? Water baptism? Speaking in tongues? I don't believe so. I believe the distinction will be loyalty to Jesus Christ. The bride will remain true; the harlot will be seduced from her loyalty to Jesus. We see both of them presented in the book of Revelation:

> *Then one of the seven angels who had the seven bowls came and talked with me, saying to me, "Come, I will show you the judgment of the great harlot who sits on many waters, with whom the kings of the earth committed fornication, and the inhabitants of the earth were made drunk with the wine of her fornication."* (Revelation 17:1–2)

> *Then one of the seven angels who had the seven bowls filled with the seven last plagues came to me and talked with me, saying, "Come, I will show you the bride, the Lamb's wife."* (Revelation 21:9)

In these verses, the harlot and the bride are set in opposition to one another. Not by a denomination or a doctrine but by a relationship to Jesus Christ. Both are well advanced in formation in the church today. The bride is nearing completion, and the harlot is surely being manifest.

We must closely guard our relationships with Christ. Some people say you should always stay in your present church. I don't counsel one way or the other. Preachers really have no authority to tell individual believers that. Just ensure that you do not end up in the harlot church—because many churches have a lot more of the harlot than the bride in them.

> *So Christ was offered once to bear the sins of many. To those who eagerly wait for Him He will appear a second time, apart from sin, for salvation.* (Hebrews 9:28)

The qualification for seeing Jesus appear for salvation is *"those who eagerly wait."* The key word is *expectancy*. He will come for those who are expecting Him as Savior. For the rest, He will come as Judge.

Holding Fast Our Confession

What, therefore, is required in our relationship to one another? *Exhortation* and *example*.

> *Let us hold fast the confession of our hope* [or faith] *without wavering,*
> *for He who promised is faithful.*   (Hebrews 10:23)

One of the themes of the book of Hebrews is a continual exhortation to stand fast in faith and not go back to the Law. The Hebrew Christians were in great danger of doing that—of almost giving up their profession of faith in Jesus the Messiah and becoming enamored again with the Old Testament worship and sacrifices. The writer of Hebrews continually pointed out the superiority of Christ and the new covenant over the Law and the old covenant. The book is addressed to people who had made a profession of faith in Christ but were in danger of turning back.

In fact, there are five separate exhortations in Hebrews on the dangers of turning back. Here the message is for us to hold fast and not give up what we have professed.

> *And let us consider one another in order to stir up* [or *"provoke"* KJV]
> *love and good works....*   (Hebrews 10:24)

Part of our responsibility is not merely to hold fast ourselves, but also to encourage one another and consider how we can provoke one another to love and good works. The word *provoke* is deliberately paradoxical. Normally, we tend to provoke people to bad acts, such as anger and jealousy. But we are to consider how we can provoke one another to *good* acts, to the outworked righteous acts of obedience.

...not forsaking the assembling of ourselves together, as is the manner of some, but exhorting one another, and so much the more as you see the Day approaching.   (Hebrews 10:25)

"*The Day*" is the day of Christ's return. The nearer we come to the day, the greater is our responsibility to meet together, challenge one another, provoke one another to do what is good, exhort one another, and watch over one another.

Here is where I believe the small group has a unique function. It is where we can best encourage and exhort one another. In a large gathering, the person who is really troubled or on the verge of backsliding can remain hidden. But in a small group of ten or twelve people, very little remains hidden for long. In a big group, the person who has some deep, inner, personal problem probably will never come out with it. But in a small group, as we lay bare our lives to one another and meet together to encourage and pray for one another, deeper issues emerge.

In my experience with small groups, religious Christians often come to a point where they are sorely tempted to turn back. New believers seem to have few problems, but those who are accustomed to being religious may have many. In my way of thinking, the cell group is not for a prayer meeting or a Bible study. In a Bible study, somebody can remain hidden. In a prayer meeting, people can pray beautiful prayers. But when it comes to opening up to one another, every one of us has to decide if it is really worth it. Do I really want people to know me *that* well? Would I prefer to keep my mask on?

WE NEED TO "PROVOKE" ONE ANOTHER TO LOVE AND GOOD WORKS.

This is something very much related to what we are looking at because the word that is used in Hebrews 10:25 means "your synagogue," the place where you gather together. It is not the word *ecclesia*, the church assembly. I believe it is really speaking about small group meetings where people can become honest with one another.

It concerns me that people can sit in a church for years and have deep personal problems that they never reveal to anybody. For instance, in my ministry of deliverance as a visiting preacher, I have discovered that there are homosexuals in many churches. You would be surprised how many evangelical Pentecostal churches have people with the problem of homosexuality. But it never is revealed because they are ashamed and they do not dare to come out into the open with it. I once received a four-page letter from a young man. The first three pages were devoted to getting me ready for what he wanted to tell me. The fourth page revealed that he was a homosexual. It took him all that time to get up the courage to make that statement. I wrote back and told him that there was hope, there was a way out. He wrote back and said, "You're the first person who has ever done anything but discourage me or reject me."

We need to have the kind of relationship with believers in which our problems can come out and be dealt with justly and mercifully. We should encourage one another, correct one another, but *not* reject one another. Someone once said, "Correct me, but don't reject me." This is what people are crying out for. I really believe that this passage in Hebrews is particularly relevant for the times and situations in which we find ourselves.

To conclude, let's look at a verse from the first chapter of Song of Solomon. This is the young lady speaking: *"Draw me away! We will run after you"* (verse 4). You will notice that she moves from singular to plural: *"Draw* **me**," and *"***We** *will run.*" This is a picture of exhortation and example. When the Lord can draw you, the people who see you running will want to run with you. So there is the responsibility of example in our relationship to the Bridegroom. All through the Song of Solomon, we are reminded of this example. The bride is asked, *"What is your beloved more than another beloved?"* (Song of Solomon 5:9). "I'll tell you!" is the answer of the bride. This is how we need to provoke people to love and good works.

9

PICTURE #7:
THE ARMY

*"Therefore take up the whole armor of God, that you may be able to
withstand in the evil day, and having done all, to stand."*
—Ephesians 6:13

So far, we have looked at six specific pictures of God's people in Ephesians:
the assembly, the body, the workmanship, the family, the temple, and the
bride. Now we are going to look at the seventh picture: the army. This last
picture is as great a contrast as it could possibly be to the previous picture.
What two representations could be less like one another than a bride and
an army?

For this final picture, we will turn to the last chapter of Ephesians. As in the case of the picture of the bride (in which the word *bride* is not actually mentioned), the word *army* is not specifically used here, but the implication is absolutely beyond doubt.

> *Finally, my brethren, be strong in the Lord and in the power of His might. Put on the whole armor of God, that you may be able to stand against the wiles of the devil. For we do not wrestle against flesh and blood, but against principalities, against powers, against the rulers of the darkness of this age, against spiritual hosts of wickedness in the heavenly places. Therefore take up the whole armor of God, that you may be able to withstand in the evil day, and having done all, to stand.* (Ephesians 6:10–13)

Here is fair warning that believers will most certainly face warfare. There will come what Paul called *"the evil day"*—the day of affliction, testing, and satanic pressures. Therefore, Paul said, *"Put on the whole armor."* What kind of person puts on armor? Obviously, the answer is a soldier. Indeed, the entire picture is very closely based on the battle gear of the Roman legionary in the time of Paul. The church is compared to a Roman legion, the most effective military unit of the ancient world—one that actually conquered most of the known world for the Roman Empire.

As God's army, believers are involved in a spiritual war. There has been a war between the forces of God and the forces of Satan throughout human history, but the coming of Jesus as Messiah, Savior, and Deliverer brought the conflict out into the open. At one point, the Pharisees were criticizing Jesus because of His ministry of casting out evil spirits. They accused Him of being in league with Beelzebub, which was one of the titles of Satan.

> *But Jesus knew their thoughts, and said to them, "Every kingdom divided against itself is brought to desolation, and every city or house divided against itself will not stand. If Satan casts out Satan, he is divided against himself. How then will his kingdom stand? And if I cast out demons by Beelzebub, by whom do your sons cast them out? Therefore they shall be your judges. But if I cast out demons by the*

Spirit of God, surely the kingdom of God has come upon you."
(Matthew 12:25–28)

Jesus said that Satan's kingdom is not divided, and it is in total opposition to the kingdom of God. In the last phrase, He spoke about His ministry of casting out evil spirits as the demonstration that the kingdom of God had come on the scene. So here we have what I call "the clash of kingdoms": the visible, manifested clash between God's kingdom—represented by Jesus and the church—and the kingdom of Satan and his demons.

Spiritual Weapons and Battlefield

We need to understand the weapons and battlefield of this spiritual conflict:

For though we walk in the flesh, we do not war according to the flesh, for the weapons of our warfare are not of the flesh, but divinely powerful for the destruction of fortresses. We are destroying speculations and every lofty thing raised up against the knowledge of God, and we are taking every thought captive to the obedience of Christ.
(2 Corinthians 10:3–5 NASB)

Paul said we are in a war *in the spiritual realm,* and therefore we must utilize spiritual weapons—not bombs, bullets, or tanks. These spiritual weapons are capable—through God's power—of destroying Satan's fortresses. Verse five clearly reveals the battlefield: *"Destroying speculations and every lofty thing raised up against the knowledge of God, and...taking every thought captive to the obedience of Christ."* Three key words, *"speculation," "knowledge,"* and *"thought,"* all relate to one particular realm: the mind.

The mind of humanity is the battlefield of this spiritual war. Satan has deceived human beings through their minds, taking them captive by building fortresses of unbelief and prejudice. Our assignment as God's army is to make war with the spiritual weapons that God has committed to us. We are to release people from Satan's bondage by breaking down his strongholds in their minds and enabling them to bring their thoughts into captivity to the obedience of Christ. This is our military assignment as the army of God.

From Bride to Army

Let us consider the process by which the bride becomes the army, which is really exciting. We find the process or transformation described in Song of Solomon. Here the bridegroom is speaking to his bride—a picture of Christ speaking to His church:

> *You are as beautiful as Tirzah, my darling, as lovely as Jerusalem, as awesome as an army with banners.* (Song of Solomon 6:4 NASB)

This is a rather unexpected combination—the words *"beautiful," "darling,"* and *"lovely"* are followed by the picture of *"an army with banners."* A feminine or bridal description turns into a military one! And then, in the tenth verse of the same chapter, the chorus (or spectators) offers this description of the bride (the church):

> *Who is this that grows* [or *"appears"* NIV] *like the dawn, as beautiful as the full moon, as pure as the sun, as awesome as an army with banners?* (verse 10 NASB)

The chorus (the world) is amazed to see the church appearing as an army. Notice the beauty of the picture:

+ "[Appears] *like the dawn"*—rising after a night of darkness.

+ *"As beautiful as the full moon"*—the moon in its function of reflecting the sun as the church reflects or manifests Christ.

+ *"As pure as the sun"*—with Christ's own purity and righteousness.

+ *"Awesome as an army with banners"*—again, the bride becomes the army, startling both Satan and the world.

This is the order: first, Christ sees His bride as an army; then, she also appears to the world in this way. This is why it is important for us to see ourselves as Christ sees us by looking in the mirror of God's Word. When we begin to see ourselves in this way by faith, then the Holy Spirit transforms us into what we see.

The Essential Feature of the Army of God

God's purpose in presenting this picture of the church, or the essential feature of God's army, is to manifest God's victory. In dealing with this tremendous theme, we need to see, first of all, that the Lord is a military commander and a man of war.

The LORD is a man of war; the LORD is His name.   (Exodus 15:3)

Who is this King of glory? The LORD strong and mighty, the LORD mighty in battle. Lift up your heads, O you gates! Lift up, you everlasting doors! And the King of glory shall come in. Who is this King of glory? The LORD of hosts, He is the King of glory. (Psalm 24:8–10)

We are familiar with the phrase *"the LORD of hosts,"* but the wording obscures some of the meaning for us today because we are not familiar with Elizabethan English. The Hebrew word that is translated *"hosts"* is *tsaba*, which is the standard Hebrew word for an army. It is also used of the modern Israeli army. Therefore, God is the Lord of armies. He is also a God of battle and a *"man of war."* He is worthy and capable of being our Commander. It is good to know this. To have confidence in your commander is a very important element of military life. Morale always fails among troops when they lack confidence in their commander. But we can have our morale strengthened by the knowledge that the Lord knows His job. He is a God of battle—a man of war, the Lord of armies.

THE ESSENTIAL FEATURE OF GOD'S ARMY IS TO MANIFEST GOD'S VICTORY.

Then we need to know that Christ has already won the victory. Paul said that God in Christ *"disarmed principalities and powers"* (Colossians 2:15)—Satan's entire kingdom with all its authorities and rulers. Christ stripped them of their armor and made a show of them openly, triumphing over them in the cross. The cross was the place where Christ once and for all sealed Satan's defeat. The enemy procured his own defeat by sending Christ to the cross. Since the time he realized what he had done, he has been busy trying to keep Christians ignorant of what the cross accomplished because it accomplished his total defeat. (See, for example, Hebrews 2:14–15.)

Christ does not want to defeat Satan alone, however. He wants us to share in His victory and its fruits. Here we have a glorious statement:

Now thanks be to God who always leads us in triumph in Christ, and through us diffuses the fragrance of His knowledge in every place.
(2 Corinthians 2:14)

Consider the two adverbial phrases in the above sentence: *"always"* and *"in every place."* Just think about this. It leaves out no time and no place. God *always* leads us in triumph in Christ *in every place.*

The word *triumph* is a very distinct, official word in the context of the Roman Empire. If a Roman general had been particularly successful in overseas wars and had added territories to the Roman Empire or defeated dangerous enemies, the senate would vote him a triumph when he came back to Rome. This was the highest honor that could be afforded to a Roman general. The triumph consisted basically of this: The general was placed in a chariot drawn by two white horses. He was led through the streets of Rome while all the people of Rome stood on the sides of the street and applauded him.

Behind the chariot, they would parade all the general's emblems of his conquests. For instance, if he had been in a land where there were wild animals that were not familiar in Rome, they would bring specimens of these animals—maybe tigers or elephants—and parade them behind the chariot. After the animals would come all the kings and generals whom that general had defeated and taken captive. They would be led in chains in humiliation. Finally, there would follow rank after rank of prisoners who had been captured in the war. And these would be the emblems and the demonstration to the people of Rome of what the general had achieved by his victory.

When Paul spoke about Christ triumphing, that was the picture he had in mind. Christ is in the chariot, and behind Him, on display, are all the forces of evil that He has defeated. The principalities and powers of Satan and all the things that oppose God and us are being led in captivity behind the chariot.

Paul said, "Thanks be to God who always leads us in triumph in Christ." Where are we in the scene? Some Christians would picture themselves being led in chains behind the chariot, but that is the place for the enemies. No, we are in the chariot. Do you know how to get there? I can tell you this great secret in one simple word: by *faith*—you just have to believe. You can't work for it; you can't pray for it; you must just believe it. Thanks be to God, who always causes us to share in Christ's triumph. Wherever we go, we are part of the spectacle, and the whole universe lines up and applauds what He has done.

God's Requirements of His Army

Now let us see what is required in our relationship to the Commander in Chief. We looked at this verse at the beginning of the chapter, but we will go on from there.

> *Finally, my brethren, be strong in the Lord and in the power of His might. Put on the whole armor of God.... Take up the whole armor of God.* (Ephesians 6:10–11, 13)

Putting on the Whole Armor

It is our responsibility as soldiers in Christ's army to put on our armor. Paul warned us very clearly that we are in a conflict. God has provided the armor, and Paul listed six items of armor in the following verses:

Stand therefore, having girded your waist with truth, having put on the breastplate of righteousness, and having shod your feet with the preparation of the gospel of peace; above all, taking the shield of faith with which you will be able to quench all the fiery darts of the wicked one. And take the helmet of salvation, and the sword of the Spirit, which is the word of God; praying always with all prayer and supplication in the Spirit. (Ephesians 6:14–18)

In one of his great hymns, Charles Wesley talked about the weapon of *"all prayer."* So we have six pieces of armor, plus the weapon of all prayer. Of these seven items, only two are weapons of offense; all the rest are weapons of defense. But the sword of the Spirit, which is the Word of God, and the weapon of all prayer are weapons of attack.

THROUGH FAITH, WE SHARE IN CHRIST'S TRIUMPH AND ARE VICTORIOUS IN HIM.

If you look closely at this picture, you will find that you are completely protected from the crown of your head to the soles of your feet except for one place: your back. There is nothing to protect the back except your fellow soldiers. This shows that we cannot afford to turn our backs and that we had better have somebody behind us who can protect us.

Teaching and Leading a Disciplined Life

Then we need to address our character as soldiers, as Paul emphasized in 2 Timothy:

And the things that you have heard from me among many witnesses,
commit these to faithful men who will be able to teach others also.

(2 Timothy 2:2)

The basic principle of discipleship is teaching others what you have been taught. The Navigators missionary organization will point out to you that there are four spiritual generations mentioned in this verse: Paul, who taught Timothy, who was to teach faithful men, who were to teach other faithful men. This is the way of perpetuating the truth in the ministry. Teach men, who will teach men, who will teach men....

Mathematically, the implications are almost incredible. I am not a mathematician, and you would have to use a calculator, but consider this: If one man wins one man and teaches him for one year, at the end of that year, you have two men who are able to teach. Suppose each of them wins another man and teaches him for another year. Now you have four men who are able to teach. At the end of five years you will have sixteen men. But at the end of about thirty years, there is nobody left to win! The whole world has been included.

That is geometric progression. On the other hand, if you were to win a thousand people to Christ every day, that would be 365,000 people a year. This number seems staggering. However, after twenty years, the other process (of one man winning and teaching another man for a year) would have completely left behind this process of simply winning people and leaving them there. Mathematically, it works. The problem with most of us is that it means starting very small. We would rather reach out for something bigger and more dramatic. This method is smaller but more effective.

In this connection, Paul went on to say something very significant to Timothy:

You therefore must endure hardship as a good soldier of Jesus Christ.
No one engaged in warfare entangles himself with the affairs of this life,
that he may please him who enlisted him as a soldier.

(2 Timothy 2:3–4)

Military discipline demands that you be prepared to endure hardship. Comfort and luxury are not primary considerations. One mark of a seasoned soldier is that he will always make himself as comfortable as possible anywhere, whether it is in a commandeered house or in the bottom of a trench. A good soldier does not depend on circumstances and can settle down wherever he is. He is detached from the normal way of life of the people around him.

So this is a complete picture of discipleship in the army of the Lord—teaching others and leading a disciplined life.

Loyalty to Our Fellow Soldiers

What is involved or required in our relationships to one another? *Loyalty*. First Chronicles 12 lists representatives from all the tribes of Israel who came to Hebron under their leaders, in military order, to make David king.

> Now these are the numbers of the divisions equipped for war, who came to David at Hebron, to turn the kingdom of Saul to him, according to the word of the LORD.   (1 Chronicles 12:23 NASB)

I believe that this is a picture of the way God is going to unite His people. The tribes will gather together under their leaders, the "tribes" being the various parts of the body of Christ that are going to be represented under their leadership with just one purpose: to make Jesus King.

Then there is a list of how many Israelites came from every tribe, with the captain specified.

> Of Zebulun, there were 50,000 who went out in the army, who could draw up in battle formation with all kinds of weapons of war and helped David with an undivided heart.   (1 Chronicles 12:33 NASB)

These were men who could keep their places in the ranks, side by side, with an undivided heart. They were loyal and committed to one another. In a battle, you need to know that the man at your right hand will still be there on your right hand regardless of the weather and regardless of the danger. You have to be able to rely on that man.

GOD'S TRUE SOLDIERS ARE THOSE WHO CAN KEEP RANK WITH AN UNDIVIDED HEART.

This picture is what the Lord is instilling in us regarding our need for committed loyalty to one another. God's true soldiers are those who can keep rank with an undivided heart. The Hebrew means "a heart and a heart." This kind of person is not one who is sweet to your face but criticizes you behind your back! You cannot go into battle with a man like that; he is more dangerous to you than the enemy.

God is saying that we need to be loyal to one another. This does not mean that you have to agree with everything somebody else does. It does mean that you will not betray him or stab him in the back but will rather stand by him and protect him from harm.

> All these, being men of war, who could draw up in battle formation, came to Hebron with a perfect heart.   (1 Chronicles 12:38 NASB)

Keeping battle formation and having a unified heart go together. If your heart is divided, you will not keep rank. You must be a person whom the Commander and your fellow soldiers can count on to be in your place.

You must be a loyal member of the army of God.

10

THE SEVEN PICTURES AND THEIR APPLICATION

What an amazing revelation the apostle Paul had of the church! I pointed out earlier that the church is the demonstration of God's manifold, or many-sided, wisdom:

> To the intent that now the manifold wisdom of God might be made known by the church to the principalities and powers in the heavenly places.... (Ephesians 3:10)

Each of the seven aspects of God's people that we have been studying presents a different aspect of God's wisdom. We need to be on our guard against focusing on any one aspect to the exclusion of the others. It is dangerous to become one-track in our approach and see only one facet of God's people. We must grow into a complete understanding and practice of all these pictures, or we will miss out on a great deal of what God has for us!

Let's review the seven pictures of the church and their references from Ephesians:

1. 1:22   The assembly
2. 1:23   The body
3. 2:10   The workmanship
4. 2:18–19   The family
5. 2:20–22   The temple
6. 5:25–32   The bride
7. 6:10–13   The army

Now, let's go through each picture, in turn, and underline the two main lessons that we learned from each—the essential, distinctive nature of the picture and the particular responsibility that is placed on us as we represent that picture individually and corporately.

The Assembly

+ *The essential feature* is being God's governmental authority. The church is God's representative body on earth through which, by spiritual power and authority, He rules the nations and brings His purposes to pass.

+ *What is required of us?* On a personal level, respect for order. We are not fit to govern if we do not have respect for due order. We cannot govern the universe until we govern ourselves. This means order in our conduct and in our relationships one to another. Here is an area where we have a lot of work to do. Corporately, we must recognize the office (or gifting) that each person holds in the assembly. God has given certain offices in the assembly: apostles, prophets, shepherds, teachers, miracles, gifts of healings, tongues, and so on. (See, for example, 1 Corinthians 12:28.) We have to recognize the office or *charisma* with which each person functions.

The Body

+ *The essential feature* is being the agent of Christ's will. The function of the body is to do the will of the One for whom the body was prepared. As the body of Christ, our function is to do the will of Christ. He is the Head, and we are the parts of the body. Jesus depends on us as the members of His body to carry out His redemptive purposes in the earth. He is not going to preach the gospel anymore; we are going to preach the gospel. He is not the personification of active ministry; we are. We are His hands and His feet.

+ *What is required of us?* Individually, we have to recognize and appreciate our differences, and corporately, we must acknowledge our interdependence, as parts of the body. We cannot say to one another, "I don't need you." We are to be different and diverse but interdependent. The body becomes effective only when we recognize this truth. Remember, there is no such thing as an effective, fruitful "lone ranger" Christian!

EACH PICTURE OF THE CHURCH REFLECTS GOD'S WISDOM.

The Workmanship

+ *The essential feature* is that we are to be the revelation to the universe of God's creative genius! We are His creative masterpiece.

To the principalities and powers in the heavenlies, the church is set as a picture of the manifold (many-sided) wisdom of God. It represents God's creative genius at its highest point.

+ *What is required of us to be part of this masterpiece?* For each of us as individuals, this requires yieldedness or pliability; and corporately, it requires "merge-ability." If we are a word in a poem, we must be the right word in the right place, and be rightly related to all the other words. If we are a member of an orchestra, we must play according to the score. We must fit in with God's design, allowing Him to make us and place us where He wants.

The Family

+ *The essential feature* is that God the Father is the life-source of all of us and that we are together, not in an institution or an organization but in a family. Jesus is our Elder Brother, and we are all members of the same family, showing the nature of God as Father.

+ *What is required of us?* Individually, it requires obedience to the commands of our Father. Jesus learned obedience through suffering and is the "pattern Son" for all Christians. Corporately, we are commanded to love one another. Jesus calls us His brothers because God calls us His sons; and if God calls our fellow believers His sons, we have to call them our brothers. This is not always easy. As the saying goes, you can choose your friends, but you cannot choose your family. As a family, we have to accept one another. Romans 15:7 says, *"Accept one another, just as Christ also accepted us to the glory of God"* (NASB). How can we glorify God apart from being a true spiritual family?

The Temple

+ *The essential feature* is being a dwelling place for God. Paul said, *"We are the temple of the living God"* (2 Corinthians 6:16 NASB). Rather than Moses's tabernacle or Solomon's temple, *we* have become God's dwelling place—both collectively, as a body of believers, and individually; each of us individually is a "living stone" in a living temple.

+ *What is required of us?* As living stones, we are to be shaped and fitted, submitting to the discipline of God and to the ministries that God has placed in the church. When we have allowed ourselves to be chiseled and hammered into shape, then, corporately, we must be willing to take our places in the temple where we belong, with one stone on either side, two stones beneath us, and, in most cases, two stones above us, too! This is required if we are going to be part of the temple.

The Bride

+ *The essential feature* is to show the glory of Christ. Human history begins and ends with a marriage. Jesus demonstrated His unreserved commitment to us by totally giving of Himself. The church is to be the bride of Christ, to whom He is going to be united eternally at the marriage supper of the Lamb. As Jesus gave Himself without reservation to the church, now He asks the church to give herself without reservation to Him.

+ *What is required of us?* Individually, as the bride, each of us must make careful preparation to put our wedding garments in order. "*The righteous acts of the saints*" (Revelation 19:8) are the fine linen that we are going to appear in. Do you want to have an incomplete wedding gown at the marriage supper? Corporately, we should exhort one another by example. This is part of our responsibility to "hold fast" and to encourage one another to love and good works.

The Army

+ *The essential feature* is being a demonstration of God's invincible power to manifest His victory! We are pitted in relentless warfare against the spiritual kingdom of Satan and equipped with spiritual weapons that enable us to cast down Satan's strongholds in the main battleground: the mind. We liberate the enemy's captives and win this world for our Lord and Savior, Jesus Christ.

+ *What is required of us?* First, on a personal level, military discipline is required. God is waiting for us to rule ourselves, particularly in our conduct and relationships. How is it with you today? How is your personal conduct? Your family? Your financial picture? Your mind? Then, corporately, we are to be loyal to one another, totally committed to one another. As soldiers in battle, we are required to be ready to defend our fellow soldiers, regardless of the danger.

AS WE FALL IN LOVE WITH GOD, HE WILL TRANSFORM US INTO A TRUE REFLECTION OF HIS TRUE CHURCH.

A True Reflection of His True Church

Even though you may intensely desire to reflect the complete image of what the church can be, all these applications may seem overwhelming. Remember the key: While we look into the mirror of God's Word, we see our real condition. Yet, as we look, the Holy Spirit transforms us into what God wants to make us. As we fall in love with Him, He will transform us into a true reflection of His true church.

And we, who with unveiled faces all reflect the Lord's glory, are being transformed into his likeness with ever-increasing glory, which comes from the Lord, who is the Spirit. (2 Corinthians 3:18 NIV)

PART 3:

THE LIFESTYLE OF THE CHURCH

11

THE DAILY LIFE OF THE LOCAL CHURCH

Some time ago, I realized that I was teaching people the initiatory experiences that bring them into the Christian life, but then I was leaving them without direction or instruction as to how to live this life after they had entered it. Therefore, in this chapter, I will endeavor to paint a picture of the lifestyle of the true local church—not its structure, administration, or titles but its lifestyle. In other words, we will consider what "a day in the life of a true church" would look like.

Three Experiences of Initiation into the Church

We will first look at three experiences that are the gateway or entrance into the local church and into daily Christian living. Then we will look at the living itself.

Acts 2 contains the clearest account both of the initiatory experiences and the ongoing daily life of the church:

> *Now when* [the people] *heard this, they were cut to the heart, and said to Peter and the rest of the apostles, "Men and brethren, what shall we do?" Then Peter said to them, "Repent, and let every one of you be baptized in the name of Jesus Christ for the remission of sins; and you shall receive the gift of the Holy Spirit."* (verses 37–38)

That is one comprehensive answer. It presents a unified experience of New Testament salvation that I call "the package deal": repent, be baptized in water, and receive the Holy Spirit. As I understand the Scripture, with these three things, they got it all. I believe that God's will and His answer to the question *"What shall we do?"* have not changed in the least bit since the day of Pentecost.

1. Repent

The Scripture is quite emphatic: we must repent. The Greek tense used in Acts 2:38 means "to do a thing once and never repeat it." There is no teaching in the New Testament about continually repenting. A person who is living right should not have to keep repenting, and a person who has truly repented should not keep sinning! This word is very decisive and incisive in the Greek: Repent. Change your mind. Stop doing the wrong things; start doing the right things. Turn from the devil; turn to God. All this is included in repentance. It is not emotion; it is a decision.

2. Be Baptized

The second thing is to be baptized: *"Let every one of you be baptized in the name of Jesus Christ for* [or into] *the remission of sins"* (Acts 2:38). In the early church, a person's baptism in water was the official recognition that he had placed his faith in Jesus Christ and received forgiveness of sins. It was not requisite for the forgiveness; rather, it was an indication that forgiveness of sins had been claimed by that person and had been acknowledged by the leaders of the church. In essence, water baptism is the human recognition of a person as being eligible for membership in the church of Jesus Christ.

Every convert in the book of Acts was normally baptized within a few hours of conversion. In Acts 8, the eunuch on the road to Gaza saw a pool of water by the side of the road and said, *"See, here is water. What hinders me from being baptized* [right now]*?"* (verse 36). In Acts 16:29–33, the Philippian jailer was saved at midnight and was baptized before dawn. Note, also, the response of the new converts in Acts 2:

> *Then those who gladly received his word were baptized; and that day about three thousand souls were added to them.*   (verse 41)

My comment is that people who do not get baptized may have received the Word, but perhaps they did not receive it gladly. Those who gladly receive the Word will get baptized.

3. Receive the Holy Spirit

The baptism in the Holy Spirit is divine recognition that a person belongs to God. The baptism in the Holy Spirit, in this sense, is a supernatural seal placed upon a person by the Head of the body, Jesus Christ, acknowledging that person as a member of His body. Paul said, *"In whom also, having believed, you were sealed with the Holy Spirit of promise"* (Ephesians 1:13).

Both of these recognitions should come at the outset of Christian living. A person should be acknowledged by the church in the act of water baptism, and he should be acknowledged by the Head of the church by the supernatural seal or baptism of the Holy Spirit.

Four Continuing Activities

Now, what did this threefold initiatory experience lead the new believers into? In Acts 2, we find the official New Testament declaration of daily Christian living. Notice that it begins with the phrase *"They continued."* Believers pass from the initiatory, single experiences, which do not have to be repeated, into the continuing, daily, regular pattern of life:

> *They continued steadfastly in the apostles' doctrine and fellowship, in the breaking of bread, and in prayers.* (Acts 2:42)

The following are descriptions of the four basic activities of New Testament Christian living.

Activity #1: Teaching

First, there is *doctrine*, which refers to the process of teaching and being taught. The first essential for people who have come to Christ and been baptized in water and in the Holy Spirit is regular, authoritative teaching in the Scriptures. Ephesians 6:17 says to *"take...the sword of the Spirit, which is the word of God."* This directive comes before the one to *"[pray] always with all prayer and supplication in the Spirit"* (verse 18). Before you move into life in the Spirit, you must take hold of the Word of God. This is the divine order, because you are open to a whole new range of problems, temptations, and difficulties once you are baptized in the Holy Spirit. This was precisely the experience of Jesus after the Spirit came upon Him. When He was tempted by the devil, Jesus used only one weapon against the enemy. Every temptation was answered with the words, *"It is written.... It is written.... It is written...."* (See Luke 4:1–13.) He utilized the sword of the Spirit, which is the Word of God. Jesus is the perfect pattern of a person baptized in the Holy Spirit yet desperately needing a sound, thorough, practical knowledge of the Word of God.

There were some five hundred believers to whom Christ had appeared at one time after His resurrection. (See 1 Corinthians 15:6.) After His ascension, however, there were only a hundred and twenty praying in the upper room. (See Acts 1:15.) Apparently, three hundred and eighty of those did not hear what He said about tarrying in Jerusalem until they were endued with power from on high. (See Luke 24:49.) The number of Jesus's disciples at this time was not very impressive by human standards, but when the Holy Spirit came, they were increased by three thousand people in one day!

What was the function of the disciples in the upper room? They provided the teaching and the authority that would immediately be needed by the people who came in to the church on the day of Pentecost. If the apostles had not been there ready to teach, there would have been chaos when the Holy Spirit fell that day.

THE DAY OF PENTECOST WOULD HAVE BEEN A DISASTER WITHOUT SYSTEMATIC, PRACTICAL BIBLE TEACHING!

This is not a theory. We saw it happen in Africa when we were missionaries. There was a sovereign outpouring of the Spirit of God, mainly on Quakers, with many hundreds receiving the baptism in the Holy Spirit. Some were actually put in prison for speaking in tongues. The American Quaker missionaries convinced the British authorities to imprison these humble Africans for speaking in tongues! Without sound teaching, many of those unfortunate people went off into the most fantastic errors and facets of fanaticism because they had no restraining, disciplinary, instructive influence at work. The day of Pentecost would have been a disaster without systematic, practical Bible teaching!

But God be thanked that though you were slaves of sin, yet you obeyed from the heart that form of doctrine to which you were delivered.
(Romans 6:17)

The word "*form*" here is from a Greek word that gives us the English word *type* and refers to a mold designed to produce a certain pattern or shape. I am no expert on molds, but whether you are casting metals or making Jell-O at home, the process is clear. First, there must be a condition (such as extreme heat) that prepares the material to make it subject to the mold. Second, there must be a mold that will produce the right shape. Spiritually speaking, salvation brings the "heat" that makes a person willing to accept a new spiritual form. The form of the mold determines the ultimate shape, and the mold is biblical teaching.

Today, we have people who have no mold and who end up like a sticky mess on a kitchen table, leaving only the mark of some undefined experience. We also have people getting into the wrong mold who end up in the wrong shape. Straightening out such people is almost impossible; they have literally had their lives formed incorrectly. Yet it is remarkable how quickly the teaching mold works. A few weeks of solid Bible teaching can produce the most wonderful change and can bring out a character and lifestyle that will withstand any test.

Speaking of the tragic situation where God's people are left without teaching, Isaiah said,

> *Therefore my people have gone into captivity, because they have no knowledge; their honorable men are famished, and their multitude dried up with thirst.* (Isaiah 5:13)

Many of God's people today are in captivity because they do not have God's kind of knowledge. I am struck by the words "*their honorable men are famished.*" Even their theologians and their leading men had nothing to give, and thus the multitudes went thirsty. In Hosea, we see a similar picture:

> *My people are destroyed for lack of knowledge. Because you have rejected knowledge, I also will reject you from being priest for Me; because you have forgotten the law of your God, I also will forget your children.* (Hosea 4:6)

Notice that the requirement of a priest is that he should know and, by implication, teach the law of God. In fact, Malachi defined this as the responsibility of the priest:

For the lips of a priest should keep knowledge, and people should seek the law from his mouth; for he is the messenger of the LORD of hosts.
(Malachi 2:7)

God rejected the priests of Hosea's time because they rejected the knowledge of God's Word. This can be equally true today. A person can enter the Catholic priesthood or the Protestant ministry while rejecting the knowledge of the Word of God, but he has no priestly ministry in the sight of God.

The statement in Hosea is so tragic and so true: *"Because you have forgotten the law of your God, I also will forget your children."* In America today, we see God-forgotten children because their parents have forgotten the law of God and have not brought them up under its teaching. This is an exact fulfillment of God's judgment.

Activity #2: Fellowship

The next basic activity is fellowship. We have to understand that fellowship is actually the end purpose of the gospel.

God is faithful, by whom you were called into the fellowship of His Son, Jesus Christ our Lord. (1 Corinthians 1:9)

"Called into" indicates destination. Fellowship is not a means to an end—it is the end. Fellowship with God and His people is where we are heading! It even precedes praying. So many of us do not realize what the church is really all about. Paul said,

These things I write to you [Timothy], *though I hope to come to you shortly; but if I am delayed, I write so that you may know how you ought to conduct yourself in the house of God, which is the church of the living God, the pillar and ground of the truth.* (1 Timothy 3:14–15)

Why did Paul write the epistle to Timothy? So that Timothy might know how to behave himself in the house of God. Paul went on to say that the church of the living God is *"the pillar and ground of the truth."* What should be happening in the church was to be no mystery to Timothy. Yet, in some churches today, it is not clear exactly what they are there for! Often, there is no fellowship at all. You cannot fellowship with the back of somebody's neck in church!

FELLOWSHIP WITH GOD AND OTHER BELIEVERS IS THE END PURPOSE OF THE GOSPEL OF JESUS CHRIST.

I remember preaching in a fine church one time, and at the conclusion of the service, the pastor said, "Now, don't hurry home. Stay and have fellowship. Shake hands with at least half a dozen people." I prayed silently, "God, is that the ration of fellowship Your people are living on? Shaking hands with half a dozen people before they go home?"

Again, most Christians do not even begin to realize that fellowship is the end purpose of the gospel. We go through religious procedures and rituals and ceremonies and programs and projects. These are all means, but do they bring us to the desired end?

The early church immediately entered into a life of fellowship manifested in two main areas or platforms. Fellowship needs a platform, and the early church had both a large one and a small one. The large-scale platform was the temple—the national, institutional place of worship for the Jewish people. The small-scale platform was the obvious, practical one that we find being used throughout the New Testament: the homes of believers.

So continuing daily with one accord in the temple, and breaking bread from house to house, they ate their food with gladness and simplicity of heart. (Acts 2:46)

Notice that, every day, they were in the temple, and they ate together in their homes. Here, breaking bread does not necessarily mean taking the Lord's Supper, though it may have included that. It means that they shared meals together every day in one another's homes, which is remarkable.

And daily in the temple, and in every house, they did not cease teaching and preaching Jesus as the Christ. (Acts 5:42)

Again, we see that their daily ration of fellowship was centered on meetings in the temple and in the homes. The first Christians continued for a time to attend the institutional place of worship, but with two qualifications: they did not compromise their testimony, and they did not depend on the institution for their personal spiritual lives. I think this is extremely relevant for us today.

Many Christians feel led to attend churches that do not feed or support them spiritually. They may do so if they do not compromise their testimony. Second, they cannot depend on the large-scale institutional type of meeting alone for their real spiritual nourishment. These early Christians certainly did not; they had a completely different life and fellowship going on in the homes.

The word *fellowship* in Greek actually means "sharing together." The fellowship of these early Christians in Jerusalem was expressed in a very intimate kind of sharing. The main thing that we share together is the Lord Jesus Christ, but these early Christians shared practically everything.

Now all who believed were together, and had all things in common, and sold their possessions and goods, and divided them among all, as anyone had need. (Acts 2:44–45)

Nor was there anyone among them who lacked; for all who were posses-
sors of lands or houses sold them, and brought the proceeds of the things
that were sold, and laid them at the apostles' feet; and they distributed
to each as anyone had need. (Acts 4:34–35)

The early Christians felt an obligation to minister not merely to the spiritual needs of their fellow believers, but also to their physical, material, and financial needs! The situation in Jerusalem was unique, for we do not read that in every city the Christians sold all their possessions. This perhaps was the wisdom and inspiration of the Holy Spirit because, in less than a generation, Jerusalem was totally desolated by the Roman armies, and Jews were not allowed to own land anywhere in that area.

So there are times of urgency when the Spirit of God will prompt us to sell out and share with everybody, but it is not necessarily a universal pattern for every situation. Without question, however, true Christians will share together with their fellow believers in every situation and need. The marvelous testimony was that there was none among them who lacked. I wonder if that could be said of all Christians today. If we shared as the New Testament believers shared, I believe it would be possible.

Another aspect about fellowship that I have discovered is that it is the place of spiritual birth. As Jesus said,

That which is born of the flesh is flesh, and that which is born of the
Spirit is spirit. (John 3:6)

Jesus was speaking about two different kinds of birth: birth out of the flesh, which produces the flesh, and birth out of the Spirit, which produces the spirit. Even so, there is much in contemporary Christianity that is born out of the flesh, and all that the flesh can ever produce is flesh. Only what is born out of the Spirit will have the life of the Spirit in it.

If we are not in fellowship, there can be no spiritual birth. So many times, we bypass fellowship and fail to produce something truly spiritual. We start a project, make a program, or appoint a committee, but what happens is flesh producing flesh! A program or a project is different from a birth. God is disciplining and dealing with many to return to the true fellowship that produces spiritual birth.

IF WE ARE NOT IN FELLOWSHIP WITH OTHER BELIEVERS, THERE CAN BE NO SPIRITUAL BIRTH.

Let's look at a conspicuous example of fellowship producing spiritual life. Acts 1:14 describes the lives of the believers who were in the upper room during the time between the ascension and the outpouring of the Holy Spirit on the day of Pentecost:

These all continued with one accord in prayer and supplication, with the women and Mary the mother of Jesus, and with His brothers.
(Acts 1:14)

The believers continued for ten days in close fellowship, in a fairly confined place, in prayer and supplication. That was surely a pretty searching experience. My wife Lydia defined fellowship in this way: "You're all fellows in the same ship, and you can't get off." Fellowship is not fellowship if you can back out and turn away any time you please! Fellowship demands a commitment to other people. That is where it tests you.

In fact, fellowship is compared to light:

But if we walk in the light as He is in the light, we have fellowship with one another.   (1 John 1:7)

If sin or darkness enters a person's life, the first obvious result is a withdrawing from fellowship. I have learned by experience that to live in the light of fellowship is an intensely testing experience. I conducted a Bible training course years ago in Jamaica. One sister lasted just three days before she flew back home, even after paying her fare and all the expenses related to the course. There was something in those forty-five Spirit-baptized people being together that this precious soul just could not survive. After one deliverance service, another woman said, "If I could have swum, I would have swum away from this island! I just could not stand the pressure with which I was being surrounded." It was the pressure of fellowship. No one was preaching at her or arguing with her, but intense fellowship generates such pressure that you either stand the fire or back out! I have seen many Christians who cannot stand the fire and light of continued fellowship. However, in real fellowship, "You're all fellows on the same ship, and you can't get off"!

Think of what must have been involved in ten days of continual prayer and supplication in the upper room. It must have tested every fiber of their being, because those apostles did not always see eye to eye with their fellow apostles. But the climax comes in Acts 2:1:

> Now when the Day of Pentecost had fully come, they were all with one accord in one place.

What happened? There was a spiritual birth. What came into being was the church of Jesus Christ, born (on the human plane) during ten days of fellowship by a hundred and twenty people. In Acts 13:1–2, we see another tremendous example of fellowship as the "birthing room" of God's purposes:

> Now in the church that was at Antioch there were certain prophets and teachers: Barnabas, Simeon..., Lucius..., Manaen..., and Saul. As they ministered to the Lord and fasted, the Holy Spirit said, "Now separate to Me Barnabas and Saul for the work to which I have called them."

Out of the fellowship of these five men waiting upon God with prayer and fasting was born what we call "foreign missions." This was the first occasion in which a church sent forth people specifically to bring the gospel to the unevangelized. On previous occasions, it had happened through persecution or seemingly by chance. Indeed, Paul's first missionary journey emerged out of fellowship and prayer, not a committee. Fellowship is of primary importance. If we want spiritual birth, we have to be in the place where it occurs. Oh, how I long to see true spiritual birth rather than a dressing up of the flesh! However, having been a missionary on more than one field, I would say it is much easier for the flesh to sit in fifteen committee meetings than it is to have one day of fellowship. In fact, I have never been in so many committee meetings as when I was a missionary!

I used to say to my fellow missionaries in Africa, "All we do is scramble out of one crisis in time to tumble into the next." One day, we had a meeting to solve the various insoluble problems we faced. The meeting started at dawn and went on hour after hour. Meanwhile, all the missionaries' children were rampaging over the mission compound and getting into trouble. About mid-afternoon, my wife Lydia said to the rest, "You carry on in the meeting; we're going to go have a meeting for the children." And so, we had a meeting for the children! Two of the real problem children received the baptism in the Holy Spirit, and one of them subsequently entered full-time ministry. It was revolutionary. We were picturing ourselves as the saviors of Africa when, in actual fact, we could not control our own children. We were neglecting the basic picture of waiting on God together in real fellowship. Committees will never produce what fellowship can.

COMMITTEES WILL NEVER PRODUCE WHAT FELLOWSHIP CAN.

Activity #3: Eating Together

The basic form of fellowship is very simple: it is eating together. This is so simple that people overlook it. We see a picture of it in Acts when Paul spent seven days in the city of Troas:

"Now on the first day of the week, when the disciples came together to break bread, Paul, ready to depart the next day, spoke [or preached] to them and continued his message until midnight" (Acts 20:7). Again, the language implies it was a normal thing for them to eat together. In their homes, around their tables, they praised the Lord, prayed, and shared the Word of God.

When God opened my eyes to the fact that eating together was an activity of fellowship, I was astonished to see how much there was in the book of Acts about eating together. As a Pentecostal, I had come to think of food as a pretty unspiritual thing, and eating together as the mark of the carnal church. I had once heard a preacher say, "They have gone from the upper room to the supper room." In fact, they *did* go from the upper room to the supper room, and they continued eating together regularly. It is a remarkable thing.

There is much significance in eating together on a regular basis. We discovered this truth in Africa where, theoretically, there was no barrier between black and white. Of course, there was a very deep split that troubled my wife and me. Eventually, we decided to invite the Africans to meet in our home, which was somewhat socially revolutionary. We discovered that this fellowship changed the whole relationship.

Later on, we would go down twice a week to eat with our students in their dining hall. We did not enjoy the food, but we found it made a completely new relationship between them and us. This is so scriptural. And, according to Eastern custom, when you eat with a person, you have committed yourself to him. You must not then be disloyal to him. It was equivalent to entering into a kind of covenant. If you partook of a man's hospitality, you put yourself under an obligation to him that only the most base and unworthy would ever violate. Part of Judas's guilt was that he first ate bread with Jesus and then betrayed Him. Psalms gives this dramatic prophecy of the betrayal of Jesus:

> *Even my own familiar friend in whom I trusted, who ate my bread, has lifted up his heel against me.* (Psalm 41:9)

Jesus Himself referred to this passage in John 13:18, shortly before Judas left to betray Him. *"I do not speak concerning all of you. I know whom I have chosen; but that the Scripture may be fulfilled, 'He who eats bread with Me has lifted up his heel against Me.'"* Again, this is the height of treason and treachery—to eat with a man and then betray him. The purpose for which God brings His people together in fellowship around the table is that we will be loyal to one another from then onward. We will not eat together with someone, say, "God bless you, brother," and then walk out and start gossiping about him around the neighborhood. If we do, we are acting like Judas, though obviously not in the same degree.

I can picture this act of eating together including the Lord's Supper. In fact, the roots of the Lord's Supper are in the Passover meal, which was indeed a whole meal enjoyed over extended fellowship. When we take the Lord's Supper, we are renewing our covenant with Jesus and with everybody else who partakes with us. We are pledging our loyalty to Him and to one another. Severe judgments are pronounced on those who take the Lord's Supper unworthily, precisely because it is a covenant meal. (See 1 Corinthians 11:27–32.) To betray a man with whom you eat *and* take the Lord's Supper is extremely dangerous. It is like looking a man in the face, waiting until he turns around, and stabbing him in the back. That is how it is viewed by biblical standards.

We see Paul's concern that this fellowship of eating together be handled correctly:

> *Therefore when you come together in one place, it is not to eat the Lord's Supper. For in eating, each one takes his own supper ahead of others; and one is hungry and another is drunk.*
>
> (1 Corinthians 11:20–21)

The Corinthian church was enthusiastic but sometimes a little blunted in their perceptions. Recall that they could be happy with the Lord's blessing upon them, even when there was gross sexual immorality in their midst. (See 1 Corinthians 5:1–2.) Apparently, they also had a very strange practice in which everybody brought his own food, and one would start eating while another was hungry. One would drink too much wine while another had nothing at all to drink.

THE FIRST AND PRIMARY OUTREACH OF THE LOCAL CHURCH IS PRAYER.

These very verses from 1 Corinthians 11 prove that the church at Corinth regularly ate together. They did not do it correctly, but at least they did come together. This was a natural form of fellowship. Paul did not criticize the fellowship, although he wouldn't have condoned the drunkenness. He was saying, "Don't imagine that this type of fellowship, in itself, is taking the Lord's Supper." Let's have fellowship around the table and do it as a church family, sharing as we eat together.

This is a totally different picture from sitting in pews and calling it fellowship. You cannot eat together with people and have the same attitude toward them. It changes you, it changes them, it changes relationships, and it changes the atmosphere. Consider this beautiful picture that gives us the "final product" of Acts 2:

> So continuing daily with one accord in the temple, and breaking bread from house to house [or eating their meals at home], they ate their food with gladness and simplicity of heart, praising God and having favor with all the people. (Acts 2:46–47)

Here is a picture of the church walking in victory, living in the Spirit and in perfect fellowship. Where was it effective? In their homes. Every meal table became a place of fellowship, a place of prayer, and a place of praise. The unbelievers did not see them in the temple because the unbelievers did not go to the temple. They saw them in their homes, and what they saw made them want what these believers had.

There isn't much happiness in many people's homes today. A really happy home, where family members enjoy one another and praise the Lord, will stand out! People will say, "What's going on there?" If the only place you display your wares is in the church building, most unbelievers will never see what you have. In Matthew 5:15–16, Jesus said that we are not to hide our light under a basket, and the biggest basket we seem to hide under today is the roof of the church building!

Activity #4: Prayer

Fourth, while the first need of the local church is teaching, the first and primary *outreach* of the local church is prayer. After a congregation is properly taught, the ministry of prayer should emerge as believers come together in the name of the Lord Jesus Christ. It is an outreach that proceeds from the teaching.

> *Therefore I exhort first of all that supplications, prayers, intercessions, and giving of thanks be made for all men.* (1 Timothy 2:1)

Paul was giving instructions to Timothy about the conduct of the affairs of a local church, and he said, "*First of all....*" The primary ministry of a local congregation is offering supplications, prayers, intercessions, and the giving of thanks. God expects the church to be a center of prayer, a powerhouse from which effective intercessory prayer goes forth into the world. If the church were fulfilling this function, its relationship to the world would be very different. If you pray for people enough, they feel something in you that causes them to respond to you. If you serve them without prayer, their attitude toward you is vastly different.

> [The Lord said,] "*Even them* [foreigners and those who feel rejected] *I will bring to My holy mountain, and make them joyful in My house of prayer. Their burnt offerings and their sacrifices will be accepted on My altar; for My house shall be called a house of prayer for all nations.*" (Isaiah 56:7)

God's house is to be called *"a house of prayer for all nations."* His people are made joyful in His house of prayer with a joy that stands the test of tribulation. There are other types of joy that Christians enter into that may not stand the test. But when we let God make us joyful in the house of prayer, we are truly established.

When I was converted out of complete ignorance to the things of God (though I had been a member of a church for twenty-five years), the thing that I liked best and never wanted to miss was the prayer meeting. This was totally alien to my natural character. I remember once, as an unbeliever, hearing about some people going to a prayer meeting. I had never been to a prayer meeting in my life and did not know what one was. However, when I understood that they were going to spend one hour in a prayer meeting, I thought, "How could people ever think of enough to pray about for one hour?" When I was saved and baptized in the Holy Spirit, I soon understood how a person could pray for long periods of time. I must say, God made me joyful in His house of prayer.

Let's return to 1 Timothy 2, where we see that the first specific topic for prayer is *"for kings and all who are in authority"* (verse 2). The first prescribed topic of prayer in the local congregation is for those who are in civil authority, not for the preachers or the missionaries or the sick. I have asked some congregations, "How many of you in the last week have even once prayed intelligently for the head of your government and its affairs?" Very rarely, you see 20 percent of the people respond. We are missing the first priority.

My dear friend, the late Don Basham, first heard me preach about this in Australia, as I asked, "How many of you pray regularly for the Queen and all the rulers of this Commonwealth?" About five out of the hundred and fifty people present rather timidly slipped their hands up, and Don was not one of them! When he heard me preach about a year later, he said, "Brother, you'll never catch me again! I was caught once, but never again. In our family, we pray for the rulers every day."

So he caught the message. Here is where the majority of professing Christians are still grossly at fault. They criticize by the hour but pray very little for the leaders they criticize. I tell people frequently, "If you would spend the time praying instead of criticizing, you would have much less to criticize." In fact, the people you criticize may be much more faithful in their jobs than you are in yours. If our rulers were not more faithful in administrating the nations than the Christians are in praying for them, we would be headed for chaos.

THE BASIC REQUIREMENT OF EFFECTIVE CORPORATE PRAYER IS HARMONY AMONG BELIEVERS.

Romans 13:1 simply states, *"The powers that be are ordained of God"* (KJV). Secular authority is ordained by God, but it is our business to see that it is directed the way God desires through our prayers. It is because of God's mercy and provision that we have secular rules and authority, without which there would be great disorder and confusion. Our responsibility is to pray for our government.

Let me say here that prayer is not a way of getting God to do what you want Him to do. Rather, it is the way to get to the place where you know God is going to do what you are asking Him to do. After coming to this place of confidence, telling Him what you desire is a small matter.

Let us also note the relationship between fellowship and prayer:

Again I say to you that if two of you agree on earth concerning anything that they ask, it will be done for them by My Father in heaven. For where two or three are gathered together in My name, I am there in the midst of them. (Matthew 18:19–20)

Where two or three have been brought together by the Holy Spirit to meet around Christ Himself, Christ promises to show up on their behalf. The basic requirement of effective corporate prayer is harmony. The Greek word for *agree* is *sumphano*, from which we get the English word *symphony*. It means "blending together in harmony." If two people harmonize, their prayers are irresistible.

The devil does not fear prayer meetings in the least bit because most of the prayers that are offered never get above the ceiling! God does not even hear them because He has strict requirements about the type of prayers He will hear. What the devil really fears is two people harmonizing. But remember that being almost in harmony is not harmony. There is nothing more grating than two instruments or voices that are almost in harmony. When we harmonize and meet the other requirements of prayer, we fulfill a necessary component of church life. Without it, we will fall short of all that God has for the church.

12

THE CORPORATE GATHERING

While the New Testament acknowledges the regular fellowship of believers in their homes, it never allows us to rest content with this alone. It encourages the corporate church to meet together. In this chapter, I will describe eight different purposes for which the believers in an area come together. The following points summarize and put into specific context many of the principles and truths we have been learning about the church and how we can apply them to our lives today.

Purposes for Which Believers Come Together

1. To Edify Each Other

> *How is it then, brethren? Whenever you come together, each of you has a psalm, has a teaching, has a tongue, has a revelation, has an interpretation. Let all things be done for edification.* (1 Corinthians 14:26)

The purpose of the gathering, as presented by Paul, is for all the believers to edify each other through prayer, worship, and the exercise of their particular gifts and ministries. It is all about mutual edification. Every time you gather with your fellow believers, therefore, imagine yourself as being "on duty" to encourage them. You are to draw from your spiritual gifts and your current devotional life to help build them up spiritually.

2. To Eat the Lord's Supper

The second purpose, as we have recently seen, is for the believers to fellowship around a meal and partake of the Lord's Supper together. This must be a time of corporate unity and not individual selfishness.

> *What! Do you not have houses to eat and to drink in? Or do you despise the church of God and shame those who have nothing? What shall I say to you? Shall I praise you in this? I do not praise you. For I received from the Lord that which I also delivered to you.... Therefore, my brethren, when you come together to eat, wait for one another.*
> (1 Corinthians 11:22–23, 33)

We can see here that everyone is important. We all know the feeling of arriving late to dinner and finding out that it has already started. How honored we would feel if everyone waited to eat until we arrived. Such was to be the spirit of even huge gatherings of several thousand believers. Paul was saying, "Wait! Hold the food until every brother or sister has arrived. How can we enjoy ourselves if they are not all here?"

This was indeed a large meeting, one that could never fit in a home, for Paul said, *"Do you not have houses to eat and to drink in?"* Here we have a gathering together around a meal and the Lord's Supper that centered on the mutual affirmation and edification of the corporate body of Christ.

3. To Be Taught by Mobile Ministries

In Acts 21, Paul visited Jerusalem after many years' absence. James and the other brethren in Jerusalem said, in effect, "Now we must have a meeting and let you minister to the whole congregation."

> *And when they heard it, they glorified the Lord. And they said to [Paul], "You see, brother, how many myriads [ten thousands] of Jews there are who have believed, and they are all zealous for the law; but they have been informed about you that you teach all the Jews who are among the Gentiles to forsake Moses, saying that they ought not to circumcise their children nor to walk according to the customs. What then? The assembly must certainly meet, for they will hear that you have come."* (Acts 21:20–22)

A mobile ministry had been directed by the Holy Spirit to the city of Jerusalem in the person of Paul, and the whole church in Jerusalem was to receive the benefit of this apostolic ministry.

THE PURPOSE OF CORPORATE GATHERING IS FOR BELIEVERS TO EDIFY ONE ANOTHER.

It is the responsibility of the local leaders to call the entire church together and make available to them the mobile ministry. The mobile ministries of the apostle, prophet, evangelist, and teacher are to take a place in corporate gatherings as the city leadership invites them. Obviously, these ministries would impact church gatherings in a powerful way, and we need their spiritual instruction and encouragement.

4. To Hear First-Person Reports of Mobile Ministries

We see such a report given by Paul to his "sending church" in Antioch:

From there they sailed to Antioch, where they had been commended to the grace of God for the work which they had completed. Now when they had come and gathered the church together, they reported all that God had done with them, and that He had opened the door of faith to the Gentiles.   (Acts 14:26–27)

Imagine a gathering of at least fifteen thousand people who had not seen Paul for two to three years!

As we have seen, when a local church sends out a ministry, it is answerable to that congregation. Even Paul and Barnabas as apostles had to give an account of their stewardship. It is an exciting and critical part of church life that local people be connected to world missions. The Great Commission must become part of the understanding and lifestyle of every congregation.

5. To Read Letters from Mobile Ministries

Often, Paul and the other apostles could not go to a city but would write a letter with the directions and instructions that the particular congregation in that city needed. Fifty percent or more of the early Christians were illiterate and could not read the letter for themselves. How was it communicated to them? The letter would be the focal point of a meeting of the whole congregation. The local elders would call all the believers together and read the letter aloud slowly. No doubt, they read it out twice or three times. The people might also have had the opportunity to say, "I didn't understand that. Read it again. What did he mean?"

Sometimes, letters were shared among churches in different cities. Paul wrote to the Colossians,

Now when this epistle is read among you, see that it is read also in the church of the Laodiceans, and that you likewise read the epistle from Laodicea. (Colossians 4:16)

Colossae and Laodicea were neighboring cities and had similar types of problems. Paul did not want to give his advice and counsel to just one church, so he said, "When this letter arrives at Colossae, it will be read among you, and when you've finished it, send it to the church at Laodicea and let it be read there. I've also sent a letter to the church at Laodicea, so when it comes, read it, too." Paul confidently anticipated that the whole group of believers would be called together in each city to hear the letters he had written to them.

So far, we see a fascinating picture of the corporate gathering of a New Testament church. We have a gathering centered on mutual edification and the sharing of a meal that might also include the ministry, report, or instruction (even by letter) of a mobile ministry. Now, there are three other purposes for such gatherings.

6. *To Settle Issues of Doctrine and Practice*

An important reason they gathered together was to settle issues of doctrine and practice. Oh, how this needs to be done to settle unresolved doctrinal issues today!

The fifteenth chapter of Acts is devoted to the discussion of what Gentiles must do to be recognized as Christians. Some of the believing Pharisees were saying, "They have to become proselytes. They have to come under the law of Moses and be circumcised. If they keep the Law, then we will acknowledge their faith in the Messiah." But Paul and Barnabas said, "No, it doesn't have to be that way." So the apostles and elders, and then the whole church in Jerusalem, met to consider and settle the question.

Then it pleased the apostles and elders, with the whole church, to send chosen men of their own company to Antioch with Paul and Barnabas.... (Acts 15:22)

The entire congregation came together. When they arrived at a decision, they sent Paul and Barnabas to communicate it to the believers in question. They arrived at a very basic fourfold code of conduct, instead of the incredibly complex law of Moses: to abstain from things polluted by idols, from things strangled, from blood, and from fornication. That is all that would be required of Mosaic observance for Gentile believers coming to the Lord Jesus. I believe true spirituality always opts for simplicity instead of complexity. Now, let's read these beautiful verses:

> *It seemed good to us, being assembled with one accord.... For it seemed*
> *good to the Holy Spirit, and to us....*   (Acts 15:25, 28)

This group of believers had arrived at absolute unanimity on what the Holy Spirit required. The principle is that matters affecting doctrine and practice relating to every believer should be settled in the entire congregation. The apostles and elders held preliminary discussions and arrived at what they considered to be the mind of the Lord, but they let it be ratified by the whole congregation.

7. To Maintain Discipline and Standards of Behavior

The church also came together in matters of discipline and standards of behavior. For example, in the case of sexual immorality in the Corinthian church, Paul felt the issue could not be ignored. For the sake of preserving purity in the church, he demanded that it be brought out in front of the whole congregation:

> *It is actually reported that there is sexual immorality among you, and*
> *such sexual immorality as is not even named among the Gentiles; that*
> *a man has his father's wife! And you are puffed up, and have not rather*
> *mourned, that he who has done this deed might be taken away from*
> *among you. For I indeed, as absent in body but present in spirit, have*
> *already judged (as though I were present) him who has so done this*
> *deed. In the name of our Lord Jesus Christ, when you are gathered*
> *together, along with my spirit, with the power of our Lord Jesus Christ,*

deliver such a one to Satan for the destruction of the flesh, that his spirit
may be saved in the day of the Lord Jesus.   (1 Corinthians 5:1–5)

Without question, Paul anticipated the whole congregation coming together as his letter was read. Judgment would be rendered so that the man might be brought to repentance and his soul eternally saved. How different it would be today if we gathered the church and dealt corporately and directly with extreme sin, especially in the lives of Christian leaders. This is part of the lifestyle of the true church.

8. To Settle Disputes Between Believers

One other reason the whole local church gathers was presented by Jesus Himself:

Moreover if your brother sins against you, go and tell him his fault
between you and him alone. If he hears you, you have gained your
brother. But if he will not hear, take with you one or two more, that "by
the mouth of two or three witnesses every word may be established."
And if he refuses to hear them, tell it to the church. But if he refuses
even to hear the church, let him be to you like a heathen and a tax col-
lector.   (Matthew 18:15–17)

We see again the need for a corporate gathering when someone refuses all previous steps to reconcile a dispute. Anyone who refuses to accept the decision of the local congregation in such matters is no longer to be treated as a Christian. The only way to make this effective is by having the entire church in agreement, so they all need to gather and come into the type of agreement pictured in the following verses:

Assuredly, I say to you, whatever you bind on earth will be bound
in heaven, and whatever you loose on earth will be loosed in heaven.
Again I say to you that if two of you agree on earth concerning anything
that they ask, it will be done for them by My Father in heaven. For
where two or three are gathered together in My name, I am there in the
midst of them.   (verses 18–20)

Notice that we move from binding and loosing to agreeing to gathering in Jesus's name. This is what happens when the church comes together in unity! We have the power to bind and loose (or forbid and permit) because we are in agreement (or harmony) as we gather around His name. Our unity enforces discipline. No rebel or rebellion can stand against the unified church.

Let's sum up the eight reasons for corporate gatherings:

1. To edify each other through gifts and ministries

2. To eat the Lord's Supper together

3. To be edified by visiting mobile ministries

4. To hear reports by mobile ministers returning to the local church that sent them out

5. To hear letters from mobile ministers read

6. To settle issues of doctrine and practice affecting all believers

7. To maintain discipline and proper standards of behavior among believers

8. To settle disputes between believers

Now, where were these meetings held? The Bible is delightfully silent about this! It just does not tell us. We know from Acts 2:46 and 5:42 that believers met in the temple. In Acts 19:9, Paul preached for a year and a half in a philosopher's school. In Acts 20:8, the believers met in an upper room. The reason why the Bible does not tell us is that it is not important. Any place that will meet the need is fine.

THE WORK OF THE GOSPEL CAN UTILIZE BUILDINGS, BUT IT CANNOT BE CONTAINED BY THEM.

The first building specifically built as a church was constructed in 222 A.D., almost two hundred years after the day of Pentecost. The Jews built synagogues, and the heathen built temples, but the early Christians coming from either Jewish or heathen backgrounds did not build. This speaks to the flexibility and mobility needed for a true New Testament church. We cannot be trapped either within or by our churches. The work of the gospel can utilize buildings, but it cannot be contained by them. The daily life of the local church has to spill out past the church buildings into the everyday world.

PART 4:

THE FUTURE
OF THE CHURCH

13

YOUR KINGDOM COME

Many Christians are preoccupied with end-time questions, such as these: "What will happen to the church in the last days? What battles and confrontations lie ahead? What role will the state of Israel play?" I will attempt to address these questions in this final section on the future of the church.

First, I must establish God's goal for the present age. We will find the answer in three words from Matthew 6:10. They are part of what we call the Lord's Prayer. Most of us who have grown up with a Christian background have prayed this prayer more times than we can remember, yet we have not often realized what we were praying for: *"Your kingdom come."* The prayer goes on, *"Your will be done on earth as it is in heaven."*

So, the prayer is saying, "Your kingdom come on earth." The ultimate goal of God for the present age is the coming of His kingdom on earth under His chosen King, the Lord Jesus Christ. I believe that Christ will actually have an earthly kingdom and that He will reign as king. I believe this is the only solution to the problems of the world.

Some people say we are dreamers, that we're talking about pie in the sky. Yet, after all these years of human history, I think the people who can imagine that *man* can resolve his own problems are the dreamers. We are probably further away from resolving the problems of the world at this time than we ever have been. So how can anyone persuade us that it is going to change through man's efforts?

There is only one hope. It is the coming of God's kingdom on earth. Every committed Christian needs to be lined up with this hope.

> *And the world is passing away, and the lust of it; but he who does the will of God abides forever.* (1 John 2:17)

God's will is not going to change. If there has to be any change, it is in our wills. If we each align our wills with the will of God, if we make the purpose of God our purpose in life, we will be as unshakable and unde-featable as the will of God. *"He who does the will of God abides forever."* The crucial issue for every person is, are you aligned with God's will? Is God's purpose your purpose?

For many churchgoers in this nation, this is not so. They are involved in all sorts of religious activities, but they have lost sight of the goal, the end purpose, which is the establishment of the kingdom of God on earth.

There are a great many passages of Scripture that speak about this kingdom, and I want to give two of them. The first is from Daniel 2:44. We cannot go into the background of this verse, but it is the interpretation by Daniel of a vision that King Nebuchadnezzar had. The king could not remember the vision, let alone understand it. Supernaturally, God showed

Daniel what the vision was and gave him the interpretation. This verse is really the climax of the interpretation:

And in the days of these kings the God of heaven will set up a kingdom which shall never be destroyed; and the kingdom shall not be left to other people; it shall break in pieces and consume all these kingdoms, and it shall stand forever.

At a certain season in human history (and I believe it is very close), God is going to set up a kingdom that will stand forever. It will never pass away, and it will never be passed on to others. It will utterly, totally, finally, and completely destroy all rival kingdoms.

Psalm 72 is what is called a messianic psalm. In other words, its theme is the kingdom of the Messiah. I want you to notice two main aspects of the messianic kingdom in this prophetic picture. First of all, the essential requirement for peace is righteousness. The politicians and other leaders who talk about peace but bypass righteousness are deceiving themselves and others. There never can be true peace without righteousness.

> *MANY CHURCHGOERS ARE INVOLVED IN RELIGIOUS ACTIVITIES BUT HAVE LOST SIGHT OF THE GOAL: THE ESTABLISHMENT OF GOD'S KINGDOM ON EARTH.*

Second, the psalm emphasizes something that I think many Christians—whether they are evangelical or full-gospel—have not adequately appreciated: God's intense concern for the poor, the needy, and the downtrodden. This is a picture of the kingdom and the King:

Give the king Your judgments, O God, and Your righteousness to the king's Son. He will judge Your people with righteousness, and Your poor with justice. The mountains will bring peace to the people, and the little hills, by righteousness. He will bring justice to the poor of the people; He will save the children of the needy, and will break in pieces the oppressor.... He shall have dominion also from sea to sea, and from the River [Euphrates] to the ends of the earth. Those who dwell in the wilderness will bow before Him, and His enemies will lick the dust. The kings of Tarshish and of the isles will bring presents; the kings of Sheba and Seba will offer gifts. Yes, all kings shall fall down before Him; all nations shall serve Him. For He will deliver the needy when he cries, the poor also, and him who has no helper. He will spare the poor and needy, and will save the souls of the needy. He will redeem their life from oppression and violence; and precious shall be their blood in His sight. (Psalm 72:1–4, 8–14)

With some exceptions, humanity does not care for the poor. The majority of the governments in the world today do not care for the poor. In Ezekiel 16:49, God paints a picture of the sins of Sodom, and it is remarkable that homosexuality is never even mentioned. The sins of Sodom were *"pride, fullness of food, and abundance of idleness; neither did she strengthen the hand of the poor and needy."* Homosexuality arises out of these conditions, which is precisely what has happened in the United States and other Western nations. But notice that the main condemnation of Sodom was that they did not strengthen the hands of the poor and the needy. Basically, in the world today, two things are happening simultaneously: the rich are getting richer and the poor are getting poorer. Most of the political negotiations that take place are aimed to protect the rich.

Let me point out one other fact about this kingdom before we focus on three primary purposes of God that need to be fulfilled prior to the coming of the kingdom. In Psalm 92, the psalmist dealt with an issue that is very current: the rise of the wicked. I have lived for over eighty years, but never have I seen wickedness flaunt itself so openly. Why does God permit this? Does God care? This is what the psalmist said:

O Lord, how great are Your works! Your thoughts are very deep. A senseless man does not know, nor does a fool understand this. When the wicked spring up like grass, and when all the workers of iniquity flourish, it is that they may be destroyed forever.   (Psalm 92:5–7)

God permits iniquity to flourish; He allows a tremendous harvest of iniquity, and it is taking place in the world today. But His purpose is to destroy the wicked. I am impressed with how little is spoken from the pulpit about the judgment of God. If we never speak about judgment, we deprive the Holy Spirit of the opportunity to convict people. Judgment is an essential part of the revelation of the gospel. Jesus is the Savior, but He is also the Judge.

In Revelation 1:9–17, John encountered Jesus as the Judge. Now, he had known Him as the Savior. He had rested his head on Jesus's breast at the Last Supper. But when he met Him as the Judge, he fell at His feet like one who was dead! I think the church needs to get a vision of Jesus as the Judge.

Now, let us look at three purposes of God that need to be fulfilled before the coming of the kingdom.

The Gospel Will Be Preached to All the World

In Matthew 24, Jesus was asked this question by His disciples:

*What will be **the sign** of Your coming, and of the end of the age?*
                    (Matthew 24:3, emphasis added)

Not *a* sign or the *signs*, but *the* sign. Jesus gave a specific answer. But before He gave it, He gave a number of signs, which were indications but not *the* sign. Let us look at some of them:

For nation will rise against nation, and kingdom against kingdom. And there will be famines, pestilences, and earthquakes in various places. All these are the beginning of sorrows [or birth pangs].
                    (verses 7–8)

The establishment of Christ's physical kingdom on earth at the end of the age cannot be organized; it can come only by a birth. This parallels the experience of every individual who enters the kingdom of God: he must be born again; there is no other way. A birth is preceded by labor pains, and the more intense the pains, the more imminent the birth. I believe we are in the period of the labor pains of the birth of Christ's physical kingdom on earth.

Here are the labor pains that Jesus described in verse 7: nation will rise against nation, kingdom against kingdom. The word *"nation"* in Greek is *ethnos*, so Jesus was referring to ethnic conflict, such as we saw after the collapse of the former Soviet Union. Personally, I believe the labor pains began with World War I. From that point onward, we have increasingly seen global conflict rooted in ethnic hatred. This is indeed a sign of the end of the age!

Now, going on in Matthew 24, we note the word *then*, which occurs multiple times. This indicates that a series of situations will develop, one after the other. After Jesus indicated that these events are the beginning of birth pangs, He said,

> *Then they will deliver you up to tribulation and kill you, and you will be hated by all nations for My name's sake.* (Matthew 24:9)

I have often asked Christian groups who the *"you"* in this verse is. These words are addressed to followers of Jesus, so *"you"* is *us*!

> *And then many will be offended, will betray one another, and will hate one another.* (verse 10)

Many *Christians* will give up their faith in the face of the persecution, and they will betray their fellow believers to save themselves. This happened in the former Soviet Union and has been happening in China probably for two generations, but it will become far more widespread.

> *Then many false prophets will rise up and deceive many.* (verse 11)

The greatest single danger at the present time is not persecution but deception. Jesus warned us against deception more than He warned us against anything else. If your attitude is "I couldn't be deceived," then you are a candidate for deception. I have learned, from over sixty years of experience, that only one thing can keep us faithful. It is not our cleverness, our knowledge of Scripture, our ministry gifts, or our status—it is the mercy of God. Paul said, *"I give judgment as one whom the Lord in His mercy has made trustworthy"* (1 Corinthians 7:25). I regularly acknowledge to God, "God, if I am to remain faithful, it will be by Your mercy, and Your mercy only. Not by my cleverness, not by the languages I know, not by the Scriptures I can quote, not by my past experience of ministry, but only by Your mercy."

And because lawlessness will abound, the love of many will grow cold.
(Matthew 24:12)

The Greek word for *"love"* here is that famous word *agape*. It means primarily the love of the Christians. Why will the love of many Christians grow cold? Because lawlessness will abound. Looking back over the last twenty or thirty years of American history, we would have to say that lawlessness is abounding. It has abounded more and more until, as a matter of fact, there is really no force that can contain it. People blame the police, but the police can maintain law and order only if the majority of citizens are law-abiding. When that comes to an end, there is no way to maintain law. Unless we are on our guard in this atmosphere of lawlessness, the result will be that our love will grow cold.

But he who endures to the end shall be saved.   (verse 13)

Actually, the Greek is more specific. It says, "He who *has endured* to the end will be saved." You are saved now, but to remain saved, you have to endure to the end. Otherwise, you will not be saved.

That is a pretty grim picture. But the next verse is astonishing, it is so paradoxical. You would expect that Jesus would say, in this situation, "Hide yourself; keep out of sight; do everything you can to protect yourself and your family. Don't become conspicuous. Maybe you will make your way through." Actually, He said the exact opposite. In the light of this situation, here is *the sign*.

> *And this gospel of the kingdom will be preached* [or proclaimed] *in all the world as a witness to all the nations, and then the end will come.*
> (Matthew 24:14)

The final, conclusive sign is the proclamation of the gospel of the kingdom in all nations. Incidentally, it is the gospel of *the kingdom*. I find that many preachers preach the love of Jesus, but they never preach the kingdom. I heard a Romanian Christian say, "As long as we told people, 'Jesus loves you,' we were all right. When we said, 'Jesus is King,' they put us in prison." That is not a popular message.

The enemies of the apostles in Corinth criticized them, and they summed up the apostles' message in this way: First, they said, "*These* [people] *have turned the world upside down*" (Acts 17:6). Would they say that about you and me? Have we turned the world upside down?

MANY PREACH THE LOVE OF JESUS BUT NEGLECT TO PREACH THE MESSAGE OF HIS KINGSHIP.

Then, they said, "*These are...saying there is another king; Jesus*" (verse 7). Is that how unbelievers would sum up the message of the gospel as we proclaim it today? I think not. Mostly, we go with the approach that "God will meet your need." It is true that God will meet your needs, but the problem with this is that it leaves people with the impression that God is there only to meet their needs. This is the attitude of most American Christians today. "God is a good God, and He will meet my need." The truth of the matter is, God does not exist for you; you exist for God. The most important thing is to glorify God, not to have your needs met. There has to be a different presentation of the gospel.

The sign, again, is:

> *And this gospel of the kingdom will be preached* [proclaimed] *in all the world as a witness to all the nations, and then the end will come.*
> (Matthew 24:14)

This is a specific answer to a specific question. My subject of study before I became a preacher was logic. To me, this is just simple logic. This is *the sign*: the gospel of the kingdom will be proclaimed in the whole world as a witness to all the nations, and then the end will come.

Let me turn to a picture of the harvest in Revelation. This is a revelation that John had concerning the result of a hundred and forty-four thousand young Jewish men going out into the world with the gospel. You may want to read the first half of Revelation 7 in order to see the context of this, but this is the fruit:

> *After these things I looked, and behold, a great multitude which no one could number, of all nations, tribes, peoples, and tongues, standing before the throne and before the Lamb, clothed with white robes, with palm branches in their hands, and crying out with a loud voice, saying, "Salvation belongs to our God who sits on the throne, and to the Lamb!"*
> (verses 9–10)

Notice that there are people from all nations, tribes, peoples, and tongues. Therefore, people of every tongue, tribal background, and ethnic group have to be reached with the gospel. I believe God is jealous for the glory of His Son. In the end, Jesus will not have died in vain. There will be at least one representative from every ethnic group before the throne.

However, they will never hear unless someone tells them. In a way, the number one priority for the church of Jesus Christ is proclaiming the gospel of the kingdom in all the world, to all nations. You would have to acknowledge that, in most religious groups in this nation, this has taken a very low priority. In fact, many Christians are not even aware it is on the list. We need a tremendous adjustment. We need what they used to call an "awakening." Not for the people out in the street, not for the people in the "old-line denominations," but for people like you and me. We need an awakening. The Bible says that a son who sleeps in harvest causes shame. (See Proverbs 10:5.) Our churches are full of sons asleep in harvest.

Israel Will Be Restored

Another thing that has to be achieved before the kingdom can come is the restoration of Israel. When I say Israel, I do not mean the church. There is probably no greater source of confusion in the church today than the misunderstanding about the identity of Israel, in which people have started to apply the name *Israel* to the church. There are over seventy places in the New Testament where the word *Israel* is used. I have investigated every one of them, and my personal conclusion is that *Israel* is never used as a synonym for the church. The truth is very simple: Israel is Israel and the church is the church. God has a plan for each, and He has enough to give to both. He does not need to rob one to bless the other.

Let's return to Matthew 24, and I will point out to you a dramatic change of focus. It's as if we have had a video screen that embraces basically the whole world. Then, suddenly, the focus changes to one very small area of the earth's surface, Jerusalem and the land of Israel.

> *Therefore when you see the "abomination of desolation," spoken of by Daniel the prophet, standing in the holy place (whoever reads, let him understand), then let those who are in Judea flee to the mountains.*
>
> (verses 15–16)

As far as I am concerned, in the light of Scripture, there is only one holy place, and that is the temple area. Notice that it does not say to flee to the West Bank. So, our focus has suddenly changed from all nations and the whole world to the city of Jerusalem and to the Jewish people in the land.

This corresponds to a passage in Romans 11. Paul wrote this to believers from Gentile backgrounds:

For I do not desire, brethren, that you should be ignorant of this mystery, lest you should be wise in your own opinion [or lest you think too highly of yourselves], that blindness [or hardening] in part has happened to Israel until the fullness [full number] of the Gentiles has come in. And so all Israel will be saved.   (verses 25–26)

It might prove an interesting challenge for you sometime to find all the places in the New Testament where Paul said he did not want believers to be ignorant. In most cases, believers are ignorant of the very things about which Paul said they should *not* be ignorant.

Here in Romans, we see that, first of all, the full number of the Gentiles has to come in. A certain number of Gentiles elected by God for salvation has to be saved. Then all Israel will be saved. Israel is the only nation of which the Bible promises that an entire nation will be saved. However, you need to bear this in mind:

Isaiah also cries out concerning Israel: "Though the number of the children of Israel be as the sand of the sea, the remnant will be saved."
(Romans 9:27)

Not *a* remnant but *the* remnant. This is the remnant chosen and foreknown by God. When it says that *"all Israel will be saved"* (Romans 9:26), *"all Israel"* will be the remnant. It will be the entire nation that is left. Israel has to go through a lot before that happens, what Scripture calls *"the time of Jacob's trouble"* (Jeremiah 30:7).

It is very important for all of us to realize the special position that the Jews occupy in the purposes of God. For many Gentiles, this is a very hard fact to swallow. Most of us who are not of Jewish background have been brought up, in varying degrees, to look down on the Jewish people, to make snide remarks about them, and so forth, and even to despise them. I am not of Jewish background, and I was never an anti-Semite, but I remember that, even in my family, which was a cultivated, British family, when they spoke about the Jews, somehow there was a different tone of voice, a different atmosphere. Anti-Semitism is bred into most Gentiles. Paul said that we better be careful. He said that we are not the root but the branches.

(See Romans 11:16–24.) Remember, the branches do not bear the root; the root bears the branches. The root is Israel. There is going to have to be a tremendous change in the thinking of multitudes of Christians in this respect because God is going to judge the nations on the basis of their attitude to the Jews. Many of you reading this may find yourselves beginning to object to this idea.

WE MUST REALIZE THE SPECIAL POSITION THAT THE JEWS OCCUPY IN THE PURPOSES OF GOD.

I was talking to a young man of Muslim background who was born in Algeria and who became a believer in Jesus Christ in a dramatic encounter. He started to argue with the Lord about the position of the Jews. The Lord said to him, "It's not the Jews you're against. It's Me." And that changed his whole attitude. The Jews did not choose themselves; God chose the Jews. If it had been left to the Jews, they would not have chosen themselves. You have no idea how much they would like to get away from the responsibility of being chosen. On his first day in office, one prime minister of Israel said, "We are a nation like any other nation." It sounds good, but it just is not true. They did not choose it, and we did not choose it—God chose it. If you have a problem with the Jews, your real problem is with God.

I believe that God makes the right choice—in our lives, in the church, and among the nations. If it had been left to me, I would not have made that choice. But God did not leave it to me. In fact, there are many things God did not leave to me. For example, I have been married twice, and each time, God chose my wife for me. He made wonderful choices, and I am grateful to Him. Maybe you are cleverer than I am, but I am just not a good enough judge of human nature to make the right choice.

The choice of the Jews is God's choice, and He knows what He is doing. Personally, I believe He is the only Person who can deal with the Jews. I am not saying that to be smart; I am just saying that they are not an easy people to deal with. God says, in effect, "I've accepted the responsibility, and in the end, I'll produce what I've promised." Jesus said, *Wisdom is justified by her children*" (Matthew 11:19). In other words, what wisdom produces is the justification for wisdom's choice. God has not finished yet. Do not judge the product until it is complete.

I want to point out something to you that is extremely important for the United States of America. I am British by background, and Britain at one time had the mandate for the government of what was called Palestine. When the United Nations decided to give the Jewish people a very small strip of territory, the official reaction of the British government was to do everything short of open war to oppose it. Now, not only am I British, but I also served in the British Army, and I was living in Palestine at that time, so I am speaking about something of which I was an eyewitness. There were forty million Arabs with modern armies against six hundred thousand Jews with very few military weapons. And who won?

Britain had a vast empire, but from the day it turned against the purposes of God for Israel, the British Empire fell apart and went into decline. They had given lip service to being in favor of the Jews, but it was not the way they acted. Frankly, the American government must be careful not to follow in the footsteps of Britain. They must not oppose the purposes of God for Israel in the peace processes. Oh, they know how to talk to Christians; they know how to use the right language. That is what politicians do—they talk to every group in such a way as to cause that group to think they are in favor of them. But when you get down to facts, it may be different.

GOD WILL JUDGE THE NATIONS ON THE BASIS OF THE WAY THEY HAVE DEALT WITH THE JEWISH PEOPLE.

I believe that no politician who takes a stand against Israel can ultimately prosper, and no nation that takes a stand against Israel can prosper. The Lord says,

> *For behold, in those days and at that time, when I bring back the captives of Judah and Jerusalem* [this is the time of the regathering of the Jewish people in which we are now living], *I will also gather all nations* [goyim, meaning Gentile nations in Hebrew], *and bring them down to the Valley of Jehoshaphat* ["Jehovah judges"]; *and I will enter into judgment with them there on account of My people, My heritage Israel, whom they have scattered among the nations; they have also divided up My land.* (Joel 3:1–2)

God says He is going to judge the nations on the basis of the way they have dealt with the Jews. Whether you like it or not, this is how it is going to happen. It is in our own interest to take note of that.

Not only did they scatter them, but they also divided up their land. We need to bear in mind that, above all, it is God's land: *"They have also divided up **My** land."*

Let me return here to the history of the present state of Israel. I would have to say that Britain carries the main responsibility for dividing the land because, in 1919 or 1920, the League of Nations gave Britain the mandate for that territory with the specific understanding that they would create a national home for the Jewish people. In 1922, the British government, with one stroke of a pen, took 76 percent of the allotted area and made it an Arab state—originally called Trans-Jordan, now called Jordan—in which no Jew is permitted to live. That means only 24 percent was left. Then the United Nations offered to the Jews about 10 percent of the remaining 24 percent. Yet God intervened. At the present time, who knows? Again, one thing I will tell you is that God will judge all nations by the way they have related to the Jewish people.

Matthew 25:31–46 refers to the coming of the King and the kingdom. We need to understand that this is a direct reference to Joel 3:1–2. It is the same scene:

When the Son of Man comes in His glory, and all the holy angels with Him, then He will sit on the throne of His glory [His earthly throne—at this moment, He is sitting on His Father's throne]. *All the nations* [goyim] *will be gathered before Him, and He will separate them one from another, as a shepherd divides his sheep from the goats.*

(Matthew 25:31–32)

So all nations will be gathered before the Lord Jesus when He comes as King, and He will separate them into two groups: the sheep on the right hand, the goats on the left. The basis of the division, if you will study the chapter carefully, is how they have treated the brothers of Jesus. *"Inasmuch as you did it to one of the least of these My brethren, you did it to me"* (Matthew 25:40; see verse 45). God has chosen to make the basis of His judgment the way the nations have related to the brothers of Jesus.

The judgments are appallingly severe. Concerning the sheep, it says, *"Come, you blessed of My Father, inherit the kingdom prepared for you from the foundation of the world"* (verse 34). That is the earthly kingdom of Jesus. To the goats, He says, *"Depart from Me, you cursed, into the everlasting fire prepared for the devil and his angels"* (verse 41).

In the political arena, the supreme purpose of God at this time is the regathering of the Jewish people in their own land preliminary to restoring them to Himself. A few of us, I think, can take into account the immensity of the miracle that, although the Jewish people were scattered for nineteen centuries among more than one hundred nations under every pressure to give up their identity, they remained a separate, distinct people. In the last ninety years, they have been regathered from more than one hundred different nations. I do not know whether you can understand what a miracle that is. It is one of the major demonstrations of the control of God over human affairs that has ever taken place in the history of this planet.

My wife Lydia was Danish. She used to say that if you were to take the Danes and scatter them among all the nations, and then come back after two hundred years, you would not find a Dane anywhere; they would all have become assimilated. The Jews were scattered for nearly two *thousand* years—and some of them for longer than that. The Jews from what is now

Yemen were scattered for twenty-five hundred years, as well as some of the Jews from what is now Iraq, but they remained a separate, identifiable people and were then brought back to the land of Israel. This, in my opinion, was as great a miracle as the exodus from Egypt.

> ## NOW IS THE TIME OF OUR PREPARATION TO BE THE BRIDE OF CHRIST, OR WE WILL NOT BE READY.

In a two-year period, four hundred thousand Russian Jews returned to Israel. The Jewish population of Israel at that time was about four million. So, 10 percent of the population were new immigrants—without resources, without finances, and often in a poor state of health—that needed to be assimilated. This would be like the United States having to assimilate twenty-seven million new immigrants in two years—and the United States has far greater resources than Israel. The American government would never even contemplate such a thing, and yet it happened in Israel. Why did it happen? Because God intended for the restoration of Israel to happen before His kingdom comes.

The Bride Will Be Perfected

Another development that will take place is the preparation of the church of Jesus Christ to become the bride of Christ. These developments are not necessarily in chronological order, but in the order that they occur in Scripture, and I think there is a certain logic to this order.

> *And I heard, as it were, the voice of a great multitude, as the sound of many waters and as the sound of mighty thunderings, saying, "Alleluia! For the Lord God Omnipotent reigns! Let us be glad and rejoice and give Him glory, for the marriage of the Lamb has come, and His wife*

*[the church] has made herself ready." And to her it was granted to be
arrayed in fine linen, clean and bright, for the fine linen is the righteous
acts of the saints.*   (Revelation 19:6–8)

We saw at the beginning of this book, in the picture of the bride from
Ephesians, that when the time of the marriage supper comes, the bride will
not be making herself ready. She will *already* have made herself ready. In
other words, now is the time of our preparation. When the event comes, it
will be too late to start preparing.

In a rather unusual set of circumstances, I became a father responsible
for eleven girls, all of whom are now married. I know they were excited
about their weddings. Most women are. They take a lot of time to prepare.
They consider the kind of dress they will wear, they plan the ceremony,
they choose the bridesmaids, and they have a rehearsal. These things are
familiar to everyone. This is just a little glimpse of what it means for the
bride of Christ to make herself ready.

If you are not preparing, I do not see how you can be ready. If you are
not even aware that you have to prepare, how can you possibly be ready?
For most women, their wedding day is the single most significant day of
their lives. This is how it will be for the church, and it requires much preparation. *"His wife has made herself ready"*—not "is making herself ready" or
"is making frantic, last-minute preparations" but *has* made herself ready.

What are the requirements for the bride to get ready? I want to offer
three. You may recall some of these points from chapter eight. They are
vitally important.

1. Total Loyalty to Jesus

This is not merely a doctrinal relationship or an intellectual relationship but a heart relationship that gives Jesus first place and will not share it
with any other. A husband and wife can love one another and have a wonderful marriage, but they must be absolutely clear that Jesus has first place.
You can never let the relationship with a spouse take precedence over your
relationship with Jesus. Never. When Jesus is in His rightful place, other
things will fall into place, and this will lead to a good marriage.

In writing to the Corinthian church, Paul said,

For I am jealous for you with godly jealousy. For I have betrothed you to one husband, that I may present you as a chaste virgin to Christ.

(2 Corinthians 11:2)

Remember that, in biblical culture, betrothal was somewhat like a present-day engagement, but it was totally binding, as binding as marriage. It was not something you could break, but it was not the consummation of the marriage, either. Paul spoke of *"a chaste virgin."*

First Corinthians 6 reveals the background of some of the people who belonged to the church in Corinth:

Do you not know that the unrighteous will not inherit the kingdom of God? Do not be deceived. Neither fornicators, nor idolaters, nor adulterers, nor homosexuals, nor sodomites, nor thieves, nor covetous, nor drunkards, nor revilers, nor extortioners will inherit the kingdom of God. And such were some of you. (verses 9–11)

We need to bear this verse in mind. You can call fornication "premarital sex" if you like, but if you practice it, you cannot enter the kingdom of God. It rules you out unless you repent and change your lifestyle. But consider that, even with the background of some of the Corinthians, Paul said, *"I have betrothed you...as a chaste virgin to Christ"* (2 Corinthians 11:2). What a testimony to the power of the blood of Jesus! Through their faith in Jesus and the power of His blood, Paul could refer to them as a chaste virgin before Christ.

Then, he was concerned that we remain faithful to our commitment to the Bridegroom until the marriage ceremony:

But I fear, lest somehow, as the serpent deceived Eve by his craftiness, so your minds may be corrupted from the simplicity [and sincerity] *that is in Christ.* (verse 3)

The danger that faces us between the time of betrothal and the celebration of the marriage supper is that our minds may be corrupted from the simplicity and sincerity that is in Jesus Christ.

I have to say that I see this happening to multitudes of believers. One of the factors is what they call New Age teaching, which has infiltrated a great deal of the church and corrupts our minds from the purity that is in Christ Jesus.

Another factor is having a whole lot of theology. Personally, I am not really in favor of so-called theology. Many people go to theological school as believers and come out as unbelievers. I believe in the systematic study of the Bible, but when people become too preoccupied with intellectual understanding and achievement, they usually lose their faith. When the church becomes preoccupied with educational achievements, it usually becomes spiritually corrupted. Harvard and Yale are two vivid examples of this because they began as Christian universities. And there are hundreds more where the same thing has happened. So, we are warned to maintain the simplicity, sincerity, and purity of our faith in Christ.

> *WE MUST NOT LOSE THE SIMPLICITY AND PURITY OF OUR FIRST LOVE FOR CHRIST AND FAITH IN HIM.*

The Lord spoke to my wife Ruth and me one time and said, "You have lost the simplicity of your first faith. I want you to come back." When you are first saved, you believe that God will answer every prayer. Isn't that right? You pray for ridiculous things, and they happen. Then you become so sophisticated that you begin to reason, "Well, yes, but...." You have lost the simplicity and the purity of your first faith. Paul was saying, "I'm concerned about you because only if you remain the way you started will you be fit to be the bride of Christ."

Ruth and I used this verse as one of our proclamations:

And such were some of you. But [we are] washed, but [we are] sanctified, but [we are] justified in the name of the Lord Jesus and by the Spirit of our God. (1 Corinthians 6:11)

This is how you have to be in order to be part of the bride of Christ. You have to be washed, sanctified, and justified. You cannot let go of the simplicity of your first faith.

In Revelation 17 and other places, the Bible speaks very frankly and openly about a church called the harlot or the prostitute. What is the difference between the bride and the harlot? Remember that there is only one essential difference—the bride has maintained her commitment to Jesus, and the harlot has turned from Him. I would say there is a harlot church in the world today and that it is growing—a church of those who have abandoned their first commitment to Jesus and become involved in all sorts of unscriptural things.

2. A Heartfelt Yearning

The second requirement of the bride is a heartfelt yearning for the coming of the Bridegroom.

Christ was offered once to bear the sins of many. To those who eagerly wait for Him He will appear a second time, apart from sin, for salvation. (Hebrews 9:28)

To whom will the Bridegroom appear? To those who eagerly wait for Him, to those who are on their tiptoes in expectancy. He will not appear to anyone else for salvation except His church. My very good friend Jim Croft used to say, "When Jesus comes back, it will not be sufficient to say, 'Nice to have You back.'" He will expect more than that.

So, let me ask you, are you yearning, really longing, for the return of the Bridegroom? Are you eagerly waiting—not just waiting, but *eagerly* waiting?

3. Proper Clothing—Righteous Acts

The third condition, as we saw earlier, is to have the proper clothing. Everybody knows that, for the bride, her attire is one of the most important features. Many years ago, a couple from a totally nonreligious background got saved. In those days, they used to bring people to our swimming pool to get baptized. The wife appeared in a knit bikini for her baptism. Some people would have been shocked, but I thought, "How wonderful to have somebody who doesn't know you shouldn't do religious things that way." So we provided her with alternative attire. But what we must realize in terms of our relationship with Christ is that we will need to be wearing more than a "bikini" to marry our Bridegroom. In other words, for our bridal attire, we must have a record of righteous acts.

> "Let us be glad and rejoice and give Him glory, for the marriage of the Lamb has come, and His wife has made herself ready." And to her it was granted to be arrayed in fine linen, clean and bright; for the fine linen is the righteous acts of the saints. (Revelation 19:7–8)

It is the things you have done for the Lord that will become your attire. Now, be honest, some of you at the moment have only a small amount of material. You need to change.

In Jesus's messages to the seven churches in Revelation 2–3, there is one thing that He said to every church: *"I know your works."* He did not say, "I know your doctrinal statement," or "I know your denominational position," or "I know your theological background." He said, "I know what you're doing." And this is what is going to provide your marriage garment. It is not going to be doctrine but the things you have done for Him.

It is not always easy to serve the Lord; sometimes, the pressures are great. But the next time you are really, honestly serving the Lord, and you feel all these pressures coming against you—and I want you to know they come against me just as much as against anybody else—just bear in mind that it is all part of providing your wedding gown. You will feel different about it then.

Let's summarize, then, the three major purposes of God that have to be fulfilled before the end of the age and the coming of the kingdom.

PRAYING "YOUR KINGDOM COME" MEANS A COMMITMENT TO BEING ALIGNED WITH EVERYTHING INVOLVED IN THE COMING OF THE KINGDOM.

First, the gospel has to be proclaimed to all nations. I believe this is the responsibility of the entire church. No Christian is exempt in this area. It is not the job of a few professionals or missionaries. There are many different responsibilities in the overall task, and every committed Christian has his part.

Second, Israel has to be restored, first to the land and second to God.

Then you shall dwell in the land that I gave to your fathers; you shall be My people, and I will be your God. (Ezekiel 36:28)

Bear in mind that the purpose of restoring the Jewish people to their land is to restore them to their God. All the rest—the political and military negotiations and interchanges—is just part of the process.

There is a reason why Israel has to be regathered. God is going to deal with them not merely as a group of individuals, but also as a nation, because He made a covenant with them as a nation. In order to deal with them as a nation, therefore, He has to regather them in one place. The only place will be the place He originally gave them to live in.

Third, as we have just discussed, the bride must be prepared for her Bridegroom.

I invite you to consider how much you are really connected with the purposes of God. The next time you pray, *"Your kingdom come"* (Matthew 6:10), bear in mind that it is a commitment to be aligned with everything that is involved in the coming of the kingdom.

14

A GLORIOUS CHURCH

The Scripture says that the church for which Jesus will be coming will be a glorious church. Yet many people associated with the church today have no concept of what this means. The Greek word for *glory* is *doxo*, from which we get the English word *doxology*, meaning "that which ascribes the glory to God."

I came to New Testament Greek by way of classical Greek, and I was a student and a teacher of the philosophy of Plato. One of the basic concepts of Plato's philosophy is summed up in this word *doxo*. In Plato's writings, *doxo* means "that which seems to be, that which appears, or opinion." This definition is very different from the way the word is used in Scripture. While I was studying philosophy, I decided that I would read the gospel of John in Greek. What really puzzled me was John's use of *doxo*. I thought to myself, "How could it be that Plato used the word to mean 'that which seems to be, that which appears,' whereas John used it for 'glory'?"

Some years later, when I was wonderfully born again, I suddenly understood the New Testament's use of the word *doxo*. The reason for the difference in translation is that God's glory is His presence manifested to man's senses. It is the visible, tangible presence of God; it is that which appears or that which is seen. When I saw this, I realized how the word had come from the meaning of "that which appears" to "glory." The *glory of God* is what appears or is manifested to the senses of man.

Speaking to the Jewish council in Acts 7:2, Stephen said, "*The God of glory appeared to our father Abraham when he was in Mesopotamia.*" Abraham knew God by His visible glory. This encounter changed Abraham's life, motives, and ambitions, to the extent that he forsook all to go to the land that God had promised him.

When the Scripture speaks about a glorious church, therefore, it means a church that is filled with the glory of God. It is a church that has within it the manifest, visible, tangible, personal presence of almighty God. It does not refer to a church that is living on naked faith without any manifestation, but a church that has entered into a relationship with God where His visible, personal, tangible presence is with His people.

A church that is permeated with the presence of God attracts people. When people sense it, they will say, "What is here? I've never felt anything like this. It's different. What do these people have that I don't?"

That is the glory of God, and it is awesome. When the glory of God was revealed to Israel, the people bowed with their faces to the ground:

When Solomon finished praying, fire came down from heaven and consumed the burnt offering and the sacrifices, and the glory of the LORD filled the temple. The priests could not enter the temple of the LORD because the glory of the LORD filled it. When all the Israelites saw the fire coming down and the glory of the LORD above the temple,

they knelt on the pavement with their faces to the ground, and they
worshiped and gave thanks to the LORD, *saying, "He is good; his love*
endures forever."   (2 Chronicles 7:1–3 NIV)

God's presence was so powerful that no one could remain standing.
This is the kind of church for which Jesus is coming.

Christ...loved the church and gave Himself for her, that He might sanc-
tify and cleanse her with the washing of water by the word....
                                           (Ephesians 5:25–26)

Jesus redeemed the church by His blood so that He might sanctify it
by the pure water of His word. The blood and the water of the Word are
both needed to make the church ready for the coming of the Lord. I always
honor the blood of Jesus. His blood paid the redemptive price by which
we are bought back out of the hand of the devil. Then, after we have been
redeemed by the blood, it is the purpose of God that we should be sanctified and cleansed by the washing of the water by the Word. His purpose
is clear:

...that He might present her to Himself a glorious church, not having
spot or wrinkle or any such thing, but that she should be holy and with-
out blemish.   (verse 27)

Therefore, here are three signs that identify the church that Jesus will
come for:

1. It is to be glorious.

2. It is to be marked by the manifest presence of God in its midst.

3. It is to be spotless, holy, and without blemish.

I am deeply concerned about the present state of the so-called char-
ismatic movement—although I think that, in some ways, it is at a char-
ismatic standstill! If it is moving, I am not sure which way it is going. It's
been my observation that many charismatics pay very little attention to
Scripture—the majority of them not having read the Bible through from

beginning to end. There are truths in the Bible that they do not know are there. While it is exciting to have the gifts of the Holy Spirit and to experience the manifestations, there is no substitute for knowing the Word of God and apprehending God's promises. The promises are breathtaking, such as this one: that we *"may be partakers of the divine nature, having escaped the corruption that is in the world through lust"* (2 Peter 1:4).

A GLORIOUS CHURCH HAS WITH IT THE MANIFEST, VISIBLE, TANGIBLE, PERSONAL PRESENCE OF ALMIGHTY GOD.

Let me ask you this: How far along are you in being a partaker of the divine nature? How much have you really escaped the corruption that is in the world through lust? Jesus is going to work out these things in His church, His bride.

Only through the washing of water by the Word can we become sanctified. I would recommend to you who are leaders that you do something about this. I can remember when, in the Pentecostal movement in this country, if you got fifty people together for a Bible study, it was a large number of people, but we did take time for the Word. In most Pentecostal congregations, every Wednesday night was a Bible study night. What has happened to Bible study? In most of the places I go to now, no time is given for Bible study at all. The leaders are responsible both to teach the Bible and, even more importantly, to teach people how to study the Bible for themselves and to give them a love for the Bible. I feel so sorry for Christians who live on the spiritual equivalent of the kind of diet that is popular today: chips and fast food. There is no fast food in God's kingdom!

This is He who came by water and blood; Jesus Christ; not only by water, but by water and blood. And it is the Spirit who bears witness, because the Spirit is truth.   (1 John 5:6)

The blood is Jesus's redeeming sacrifice, but the water is the regular cleansing and sanctifying of the Word of God. The two have to go together. Without the blood, we have no access, we have no life. But without the Word, we are not cleansed; we are not sanctified; our impurities are not washed away.

In addition to receiving life and cleansing through the blood and the water, the church needs to be built. In Ephesians 4:11, we see the means by which the church will be made ready for the coming of the Lord—by the five main body-building ministries: apostles, prophets, evangelists, shepherds (or pastors), and teachers. In the next two verses, we see the purpose for which these ministries were given:

For the equipping [or perfecting] *of the saints for the work of the ministry, for the edifying of the body of Christ, till we all come to the unity of the faith and of the knowledge of the Son of God, to a perfect man, to the measure of the stature of the fullness of Christ.*   (verses 12–13)

These building ministries are given until we all come into the unity of the faith through acknowledging Jesus Christ. Unity will not come by sitting and discussing doctrine. If there is one thing for sure, discussing doctrine does not unite Christians! The only way in which we will be united is by coming together around the headship of the Lord Jesus Christ in His supreme authority over every aspect of the church. You see, the doctrine of salvation is meaningless without the person of the Savior. The doctrine of healing is meaningless without the Healer. The doctrine of deliverance is meaningless without the Deliverer. The baptism in the Holy Spirit is meaningless without the Baptizer.

When we acknowledge the Savior, we believe in salvation. When we acknowledge the Healer, we believe in healing. When we acknowledge the Baptizer, we believe in the baptism in the Holy Spirit. When we acknowledge the Deliverer, we believe in deliverance from evil spirits. In every case, the road to unity is not the road of doctrinal disputation and discussion but the acknowledgment of the Lord Jesus Christ in His glory.

As we acknowledge Christ in all that He is to the church, we are brought into the unity of the faith, *"to a perfect man, to the measure of the stature of the fullness of Christ."* The key word here is *"fullness."* Until the church of Jesus Christ demonstrates Christ in all His fullness—in every aspect, every grace, every gift, every ministry—the church is not fulfilling its calling. At the present time, we manifest to the world a pathetically small part of the totality of Jesus Christ. There is much of Jesus that the church is incapable of demonstrating to the world, but God is going to bring us into that place where the corporate body of Christ will fully reveal the totality of Jesus.

> *For this reason I bow my knees to the Father of our Lord Jesus Christ, from whom the whole family in heaven and earth is named, that He would grant you, according to the riches of His glory, to be strengthened with might through His Spirit in the inner man* [the Spirit is the one who ministers the glory and makes it available], *that Christ may dwell in your hearts through faith; that you, being rooted and grounded in love, may be able to comprehend with all the saints what is the width and length and depth and height....* (Ephesians 3:14–18)

None of us can comprehend this individually; it is only as we come together with our fellow believers that we are able to comprehend the totality of Jesus Christ—the width, the length, the depth, and the height. Paul went on to say,

> *...to know the love of Christ which passes knowledge; that you may be filled with all the fullness of God.* (verse 19)

This is a tremendous statement: the church of Jesus Christ is going to be the dwelling place of all the fullness of God! The totality of God, in all His nature, in all His power, and in all His aspects, will be manifested in the church. There is only one other place in Scripture that I know of where the phrase "the fullness of God" is used, and that is in Colossians 2, where it says of Jesus, *"For in him dwells all the fullness of the Godhead bodily"* (verse 9). In Christ, God was manifested totally, not partially. When the Holy Spirit has completed the work of forming the body of Christ, the fullness of God will be manifested in the church, as well. Never imagine that this can happen to you alone. You are just a little unit on your own. It is only as you come together into the unity of the faith and the acknowledgment of Christ that you will be able to comprehend with all believers the width, the length, the depth, and the height, and thus be filled with all the fullness of God. This is the purpose of God for the church.

God is going to manifest Himself in such a way that the whole earth will fear before Him and will see His glory:

So shall they fear the name of the LORD from the west, and His glory from the rising of the sun; when the enemy comes in like a flood, the Spirit of the LORD will lift up a standard against him. (Isaiah 59:19)

The second half of this verse relates to our situation. The truth is, our enemy the devil *has* come in like a flood. He has infiltrated every area of our national life: politically, socially, and educationally, including the schools, the colleges, the universities, and the seminaries. Every aspect of national life in this country has, in the past few decades, been systematically infiltrated by the enemy's forces.

Not only has he come in like a flood to the world, but he has also come in to the church. This is the fulfillment of the prophecy of Joel, in which the people of God and their inheritance are desolated, much like an invading army of insects desolates the land. (See Joel 1:4.) Through the centuries, the church has been invaded by God's great army of judgment: the chewing locust, the swarming locust, the crawling locust, and the consuming locust. But God says that, at this time, His Spirit will move among us. *"When the enemy comes in like a flood, the Spirit of the LORD will lift up a standard against him."*

The standard that the Spirit of God will lift up is just one Person, and that is Jesus Christ. The Holy Spirit does not lift up a human personality;

He does not exalt a doctrine or an institution. He has come to the church to do one primary thing: to lift up Jesus. In John 16:13–14, Jesus said, *"When He, the Spirit of truth, has come,...He will glorify Me, for He will take of what is Mine and declare it to you."* The ministry of the Holy Spirit within the church is to reveal, uplift, magnify, and glorify Jesus Christ.

AS THE NIGHT GETS DARKER AND DARKER, THE CHILDREN OF GOD ARE GOING TO SHINE LIKE STARS IN THEIR GLORY.

The church must acknowledge and worship the Lord Jesus Christ. The Scripture says that through faith in Jesus Christ, we are the children of Abraham. (See Galatians 3:7.) God said to Abraham, "Your children are going to be like the stars of the sky." (See Genesis 5:15.) Normally speaking, when the sun is shining, or even at night, when the moon is shining, we do not pay much attention to the stars. But when the sun has set, and the moon is not shining brightly, and when every natural source of light has been extinguished, the stars shine brighter in the pitch darkness. This is precisely how it is going to be at the close of the age, as darkness covers the earth and deep darkness the people (see Isaiah 60:2); as the night gets darker and darker, the children of Abraham, through faith in Jesus Christ, are going to shine out like the stars in their glory. (See Philippians 2:14–16.)

Here is a glimpse of the bride coming forth in her glory:

Who is she who looks forth as the morning, fair as the moon, clear as the sun, awesome as an army with banners? (Song of Solomon 6:10)

When the church manifests the glory of Christ, the world will recoil in amazement; it never will have seen a church like this. Who is this coming forth like the morning? After a night of darkness, the church will be like the rising of the sun. The bride of Christ will also be as beautiful as the moon.

The responsibility of the moon is to reflect the light of the sun, and the moon appears in phases—quarter, half, three-quarter, and full moon. It waxes and wanes, as the church of Jesus Christ has waxed and waned. Yet, when the church ultimately comes back to full moon, it will fully reflect the glory of the Son. That is what the world is going to see—a full-orbed church, completely reflecting the glory and brightness of the Son.

And the church will be as clear as the sun. Although it will be as the moon, it will have the righteousness and the authority of the Son of Righteousness, Jesus Christ, applied to it, and it will be as awesome as an army with banners. Who has seen a church that is awesome to the forces of evil and darkness, sin and Satan? A church is coming forth that is going to cause the forces of Satan to tremble and flee.

God has shown me through experience that there is one message the devil fears more than any other. It is the message of what the church is going to be, and what it is going to do to him. The devil fights against this truth more than any other truth.

This is a picture of the church as God intends it to be. Take time to let God challenge you with His plan for the church and His plan for your individual life. He is coming back for a glorious church, and a glorious church He will have!

ABOUT THE AUTHOR

Derek Prince (1915–2003) was born in India of British parents. He was educated as a scholar of Greek and Latin at Eton College and King's College, Cambridge, in England. Upon graduation, he held a fellowship (equivalent to a professorship) in Ancient and Modern Philosophy at King's College. Prince also studied Hebrew, Aramaic, and modern languages at Cambridge and the Hebrew University in Jerusalem. As a student, he was a philosopher and a self-proclaimed agnostic.

While serving in the Royal Army Medical Corps (RAMC) during World War II, Prince began to study the Bible as a philosophical work.

Converted through a powerful encounter with Jesus Christ, he was baptized in the Holy Spirit a few days later. Out of this encounter, he formed two conclusions: first, that Jesus Christ is alive; second, that the Bible is a true, relevant, up-to-date book. These conclusions altered the whole course of his life, which he then devoted to studying and teaching the Bible as the Word of God.

Discharged from the army in Jerusalem in 1945, he married Lydia Christensen, founder of a children's home there. Upon their marriage, he immediately became father to Lydia's eight adopted daughters—six Jewish, one Palestinian Arab, and one English. Together, the family saw the rebirth of the state of Israel in 1948. In the late 1950s, they adopted another daughter while Prince was serving as principal of a teachers' training college in Kenya.

In 1963, the Princes immigrated to the United States and pastored a church in Seattle. In 1973, Prince became one of the founders of Intercessors for America. His book *Shaping History through Prayer and Fasting* has awakened Christians around the world to their responsibility to pray for their governments. Many consider underground translations of the book as instrumental in the fall of communist regimes in the USSR, East Germany, and Czechoslovakia.

Lydia Prince died in 1975, and Prince married Ruth Baker (a single mother to three adopted children) in 1978. He met his second wife, like his first wife, while she was serving the Lord in Jerusalem. Ruth died in December 1998 in Jerusalem, where they had lived since 1981.

Until a few years before his own death in 2003 at the age of eighty-eight, Prince persisted in the ministry God had called him to as he traveled the world, imparting God's revealed truth, praying for the sick and afflicted, and sharing his prophetic insights into world events in the light of Scripture. Internationally recognized as a Bible scholar and spiritual patriarch, Derek Prince established a teaching ministry that spanned six continents and more than sixty years. He is the author of more than eighty books, six hundred audio teachings, and one hundred video teachings, many of which have been translated and published in more than one hundred languages. He pioneered teaching on such groundbreaking themes as generational curses, the biblical significance of Israel, and demonology.

Prince's radio program, which began in 1979, has been translated into more than a dozen languages and continues to touch lives. Derek Prince's main gift of explaining the Bible and its teachings in a clear and simple way has helped build a foundation of faith in millions of lives. His nondenominational, nonsectarian approach has made his teaching equally relevant and helpful to people from all racial and religious backgrounds, and his messages are estimated to have reached more than half the globe.

In 2002, he said, "It is my desire—and I believe the Lord's desire—that this ministry continue the work, which God began through me over sixty years ago, until Jesus returns."

Derek Prince Ministries continues to reach out to believers in over 140 countries with Derek's teaching, fulfilling the mandate to keep on "until Jesus returns." This is accomplished through the outreaches of more than forty-five Derek Prince offices around the world, including primary work in Australia, Canada, China, France, Germany, the Netherlands, New Zealand, Norway, Russia, South Africa, Switzerland, the United Kingdom, and the United States.

For current information about these and other worldwide locations, visit www.derekprince.org.

Welcome to Our House!

We Have a Special Gift for You

It is our privilege and pleasure to share in your love of Christian books. We are committed to bringing you authors and books that feed, challenge, and enrich your faith.

To show our appreciation, we invite you to sign up to receive a specially selected **Reader Appreciation Gift**, with our compliments. Just go to the Web address at the bottom of this page.

God bless you as you seek a deeper walk with Him!

WHITAKER
HOUSE